Second
Chances

Matthew Bell

Matthew Bell

First published in Northern Ireland in 2023
by Excalibur Press

ISBN: 978-1-910728-63-5

Formatting & layout by
Excalibur Press

Cover Photo by
Adrian Boehem

Excalibur Press
Belfast, Northern Ireland

team@excaliburpress.co.uk

07982628911 | @ExcaliburPress

excaliburpress.co.uk

*The author of this book has pledged to support the Friends of The Cancer
Centre, Belfast from his proceeds.*

Foreword

Sport has the capacity to stir the emotions and for over a quarter of a century I've been lucky enough to be able to tell the stories of the unique journey every sportsman and woman takes as they strive for success and the setbacks and failure they overcome on the way.

These personal testimonies are inspirational, emotional and at times heart-warming.

Very few see the athlete face a life-threatening situation but then find the strength to overcome it and make it all the way back onto the field of play.

Matthew hated it when I singled him out for an interview. It was a running joke between us when I had to persuade him to stand in front of a camera before or after a match. Which wasn't to say he was a bad interviewee, far from it, Matthew was never short of a word or two. He was one of my 'go-to' guys because if I needed a quick quote, I knew Matthew would always give me what I required.

We built a mutual respect between journalist and player that turned into a friendship and that led me getting to know his family who looked after me so well when I visited the hockey club at Banbridge.

Matthew was a mainstay of the Ireland men's squad as they looked forward to qualifying for the Tokyo Olympics and had made a club move to Germany and away from his beloved Banbridge for which he had so much success.

Matthew was on the journey that would hopefully take him to the top of the hockey world.

And then I was told about his brain tumour. Details were scarce. I would ask friends at Banbridge Hockey Club how Matthew was getting on and they would let me know. You didn't want to intrude, you just prayed for his recovery.

I had absolutely no idea however what Matthew had gone through until after the first Covid lockdown in 2020 when I asked him to tell his story for BBC Northern Ireland.

I told him that day that when he stepped on the hockey pitch again for the first time I'd be there with my camera. I had no idea when I said that at the time, if that moment would ever come.

It took twenty months after the interview in August 2020, but Matthew made it back and I was there too.

It's a story that will stir your emotions.

This is Matthew's journey…so far.

- Nigel Ringland, BBC Sport

ACKNOWLEDGMENTS

I would like to acknowledge and say thanks to my club Crefelder HTC for organising the surgeon – Prof. Scholz – who performed my brain surgeries. To my teammates, flat mates and coaching staff for coming to visit me every day while I was recovering in hospital in Germany.

To the staff of the NHS who looked after me during my time in hospital in Northern Ireland throughout chemotherapy and radiotherapy treatment.

My friends who came to visit me every week in hospital in Belfast and spent an evening doing Secret Santa in my room in place of our usual Christmas dinner.

To my family who came to visit me every day in the hospital. My parents, who moved to Germany for 6 weeks while I was in hospital there. My sister and my brother-in-law who came to visit me every week in Belfast. The last couple of years have shown me just how important family is.

Thanks to everyone who helped fill in the blanks with the short-term memory loss during my time in France at Le Touquet, Belgium, Germany and the Royal Victoria Hospital in Belfast. My parents, sister, teammates from all teams – Ireland, KHC Dragons in Belgium, Crefelder HTC in Germany and Banbridge Hockey Club in Northern Ireland, I just want to say thank you.

Lastly, to Jane. Thank you for being my rock. Driving me anywhere I needed to go before I got my licence back and standing by my side for all the milestones during my recovery. I love you and can't wait to spend the rest of my life with you.

Matthew Bell

The Worst Day of My Life

Saturday 9th July 2016 was the worst day of my life. Well, of my life so far; little did I know then, that far worse was just around the corner.

It was the day the Irish Men's hockey squad for the Rio de Janeiro Olympic Games was to be announced and I was in contention for a place in defence. Unlike all other international tournaments, the Olympics is only a 16-man squad whereas every other major tournament is 18. This is due to a restriction in numbers in the athlete village. They didn't have enough accommodation to host 24 teams, 12 male and 12 female, of 18 athletes each. In an 18-man squad there is usually 2 goalkeepers, 6 defenders, 5 midfielders and 5 forwards. Whereas for the Olympics it would be 1 goalkeeper, 5 defenders, 5 midfielders and 5 forwards. Competition for places was tight and just because I had been part of the squad that won Ireland's first ever European Championship medal the year before didn't mean I was guaranteed a place in the Olympic squad.

We were to receive an email at 8am in the morning with the selected squad that would travel to Buenos Aires, Argentina, for a pre-tournament camp and then on to Rio de Janeiro for the Games.

I hadn't slept all night, my nerves wouldn't let me. All I could think about was that email that was coming in the morning. The team and I had worked ridiculously hard in the lead up. Full time training Sunday, Monday and Tuesday in Dublin after a match for your club on the Saturday. We ate as a team, trained as a team, and stayed in a hotel as a team, so we could have meetings whenever necessary.

8 o'clock came. No email. 8:05 came. Still no email. I was continuously refreshing the email app on my phone. My thumb was aching from the incessant swiping down. 8:10 came and the email entered my inbox. I frantically opened it, not even reading the actual email. I went straight for the attachment, which always held the selected team for whatever respective tournament the email was about. The team sheet was always written in alphabetical order, so mine would have been near the top of the list. 'Irish Olympic Team of 16 + Travelling Reserves: Jonny Bell, Chris Cargo, Peter Caruth…'

My name wasn't there. I scanned and scanned. Read and re-read, just to make sure. I must have read that attachment fifty times to check, but it still wasn't there. Or rather, it was. At the bottom of the page, under the heading 'ISM Non Travelling', stating I hadn't been selected.

I started to cry. Everything, over the last few months, was worth nothing, it had been a waste of time. I'd even taken a year out of my university degree to focus on my training, and recovery from the intense training, to give myself the best chance of being selected. It would have been my final year of studying. I was studying a master's degree in Mechanical Engineering at Queen's University Belfast but taking a year out meant I wouldn't graduate with friends that I had made during the 4 years studying and living in Belfast. I was only 22 years of age at the time. I would have turned 23 at the Games. What a birthday that would have been. One to remember.

My parents knew I was receiving the email that morning. It was a Saturday, so my dad was out playing golf as he always did at the weekend. At 8:30 my mum opened my bedroom door and heard me crying in the dark. She just closed the door without saying a word. She knew the contents of the email without asking. She knew that I hadn't made the team. She also knew to leave me alone as I didn't want to speak to anyone, not even my mum.

Eventually after an hour of crying I got myself out of bed and made my way down to mum. She just hugged me. That hug lasted a good 5 minutes. It was what I needed. Dad came home from golf and joined the embrace. He could sense from the mood in the kitchen what had happened. He just said, "I'm sorry Matthew". I started to cry again. I didn't eat any breakfast that morning, which was a rarity for me.

After speaking to mum and dad, I went back to my room. I looked in the mirror and made a promise to myself, that I would never let myself feel that way again. I only had myself to blame. I obviously didn't work hard enough to make that team. I was playing the best hockey of my life and had been for the previous year, but it wasn't enough. I was adamant that one day I would become an Olympian. I would do whatever it took, to get to that level. That's when I made the decision that I wanted to play abroad, in Europe. The best leagues in the world were in Europe, Germany, Holland and Belgium were the top three. I knew of other Irish players who had played abroad, and it raised their game to the next level. I knew it would help me and I already had offers from a couple of clubs in Belgium, but my mum wouldn't let me go until I finished my degree. To be fair, now I'm glad I listened to her advice. They do say your mum is always right.

That night, a group of friends were going out for a birthday celebration. It was Rachael's, one of my closest female friends. We went to 'The Perch', a rooftop bar in Belfast. I drove as I didn't feel like drinking. My friends didn't know that I had received that email. They didn't know I hadn't made the team for the Olympics. I'm surprised they didn't suspect something, as I didn't say a word all night. I just sat in silence, listening to the conversation that unfolded. I also went home early, I didn't see midnight. I just wanted to be back in my bed, wrapped in my duvet. I cried myself to sleep. The thought of not making that team was in the forefront of my mind.

I'd never let this happen again.

GRANDA'S PASSING & LE TOUQUET

Fast forward a couple of years and my grandfather hadn't been well. He was a frail man of 85 years. He turned 85 on the 8th of May. My dad's, dad. He always supported me in everything I did. Whether it was academics, music or sport, he always backed me. He even bought me my first clarinet as I was moving to private lessons in my school, and we could no longer rent one from the education board. The lessons that I had from the education board were moving to a Saturday and that would have interfered with my hockey, which was a big no for me. Nothing would get in the way of hockey. He was very upset when I gave up the instrument. I was working towards my grade 7 but, to me, hockey was more important, and at that point I was starting to play representative hockey, which took up a lot more of my spare time.

A month after Granda's 85th birthday, the Irish hockey team had 2 warm up matches for Le Touquet, against France in Hillsborough, Northern Ireland. on the 4th and 6th of June at the home of Lisnagarvey Hockey Club. I only played one game. When the team bus pulled into the ground I sprinted to the toilet. I needed to vomit. During the match, my eyesight was causing me issues, it was ridiculously blurry, what was going on? I didn't play the second match due to my eyesight and previous vomiting.

The morning after the second match, which I didn't even play in after what had had happened a couple of days before, I woke up with a migraine. I quickly rushed to the bathroom down the hall from my bedroom to vomit. What was happening? I knew Granda was very unwell, was this causing me to feel unwell?

I soon found out that Granda had passed away a few hours

earlier - in the early morning of Friday 7th June 2019. My dad was with him in his last moments, in his nursing home in Banbridge. He had been moved there as my Granny was in her own nursing home, as she was suffering from dementia. My Granny and Granda both had fallen at home and an ambulance had to be called for them. Granda had fallen in the kitchen and my Granny had tried to help him back to his feet, causing her to fall as well. My Granny never returned home, she was placed in a care home for Dementia. My Granda moved back home, and we had to move a bed downstairs into the dining room for him as he was too frail to make it up the stairs by himself. My Granda had to be placed into a care home also, after a week, as he wasn't capable of looking after himself. He needed my Granny to look after him, make his food for him, clean the house but she wasn't able to do so any longer.

The next day, the day after his passing, and the day before his funeral, I woke up with a migraine again. I quickly ran to the bathroom, I needed to throw up, again. My parents put it down to grief, from losing my grandfather. Little did my family and I know, something far more serious and sinister was starting to unfold and manifest itself.

That night I went to 'The Pot Belly' restaurant with my then girlfriend, Lauren, for a meal. My old workplace, where I was always treated like royalty, as I had spent 6 years there as a barman and a waiter. I was heading to France on Monday – two days later - for an international tournament with the Irish team. It was the first stage of qualification for the Olympic Games – time to right a wrong. When I came home from the restaurant, I rushed to the toilet. I needed to vomit again. Was it the food? It couldn't have been, not from The Pot Belly.

The next day, Sunday 9th June, was Granda's funeral. The same thing happened that morning. I woke up with a banging headache and the need to vomit. I made my way to the bathroom like the previous mornings. It was becoming a routine, but not by choice and not one I wanted. After the funeral my family went to 'The Pot Belly' for Sunday lunch. My parents, sister, brother-in-law, aunt, uncle and cousins. Lauren joined us later for the food as she was working and couldn't come to the funeral. We were treated like royalty, again. A private dining room for the family and a free bottle of prosecco, to make a toast to Granda. I didn't vomit after, it definitely wasn't the food from the night before.

Mum decided to book me an appointment for the GP. She was worried about me, as any mother would be of their child. To see if the doctor could figure out why I was vomiting and having these migraines.

I went with the Ireland team to Le Touquet on the 10th of June for our World Series. It was the competition we needed to reach the final of, to get an Olympic qualifier later in the year. We were the highest ranked team, 11th in the world. France our closest rivals were 15th in the world and the hosts, giving them the home advantage. Our first match was against Scotland, and we won 4-2. We then surprisingly lost to Egypt 2:1. A team ranked 10 places lower than us in the world rankings.

The migraines and vomiting had stopped. I was on the phone one night to my mum. "You can cancel the doctor's appointment, mum. I'm not throwing up anymore and the migraines have stopped", I said to her. She did cancel the appointment.

I wonder to this day if I had gone to see the doctor would they have suspected anything? Would they have sent me for a CT scan, or an MRI? Would they have caught what was coming down the line early on?

Our third game of the tournament, on the 18th was against

Singapore. A big day for me as it was my 100th match for my country which we won 11-0. My Granda would have been proud to see me pull on the green jersey for the 100th time, but sadly that wasn't meant to be, but he must have been looking over myself and the team with us achieving a result like that.

Thankfully my parents had made the trip to watch the tournament and see me gain my 100th cap. We then proceeded to the semi-final to play against Korea. This was the big one; the winners go through to the Olympic qualifiers but for the losers, it's another 4 years wait. We won 4:2. That meant we qualified for the Olympic qualifier later in the year and France awaited us in the final. We lost the final 3:1. We didn't deserve to win that game for the way we played, but we had achieved what we had went to achieve. A chance to qualify for the Tokyo 2020 Olympics.

Mum, Dad and I after my 100th cap

Dad and I embracing after the semi-final win and qualifying for the Olympic Qualifier

Mum and I embracing after the same match

After Le Touquet I went to the opticians. To see my dad's cousin, Richard. He checked my eyes and he found that I had what's known as an 'astigmatism'. I needed glasses. It made sense, it explained my blurry, distorted vision. I got glasses to help and what a difference they made. I received my glasses and ordered contact lenses for playing hockey in. Finally, normality was resuming. Whatever had been going on, maybe it was all over.

In July, after a holiday, I received my contact lenses. 'Great!' I thought, everything will go back to normal now. We played one match against Scotland in Glasgow, winning 2:1. The lenses didn't work. They moved about in my eyes, so they didn't settle, which meant my eyesight was still blurry. What a let-down. I was expecting normality and it was far from that. I could barely stop the ball. I always prided myself on my hockey basics, being able to pass and stop the ball when it came into my vicinity. Speaking to my teammates, I could barely stop the ball, or make a 5-yard pass. Something I could normally do with my eyes closed. I can imagine I was very frustrated with myself, but I can't remember.

In early August we had a warmup tournament in Barcelona before the European Championships which were to be held in Antwerp. We played a 4-Nations against England, Malaysia and Spain. I barely played because I kept taking myself off, which wasn't like me at all, because of my blurry vision. Not surprisingly, I didn't get selected for the European Championships. The first tournament since the Rio de Janeiro Olympics I hadn't made. A lot of questions were asked by people outside the squad. 'Why isn't Beller picked?'. 'Beller' is my nickname and has been since I started Banbridge Academy, the secondary school I went to. I got messages asking me why I didn't get selected, but I didn't reply. I was ashamed of myself and didn't want to face anyone. I knew why I wasn't picked. I was playing some of the worst hockey, if not the worst hockey of the last few years of my hockey career.

Time in Belgium

After two happy years playing in the Bundesliga for Crefelder HTC in Germany, I decided the time was right for me to move on and experience hockey in a different country. I arrived in Belgium on the 20th of August. I had signed a pre-contract with European club, KHC Dragons, one of the best club sides in European hockey. I was recommended to them by an Irish teammate of mine, Shane O'Donoghue, who had already played for them and was to join us after the European Championships.

I flew from Dublin to Antwerp and my housemate to be, Luke, came to pick me up. An Australian guy who also was a defender. We were supposed to be centre back partners. We would form a great friendship in the short time I was in Belgium. When he picked me up at the airport, hockey bags and suitcases in tow we went back to the house, the 'hockey house', as it was known, as the club owned it. It was a 5-minute drive from the clubhouse and pitches. We went back to meet our other housemate, Koen Bakhuis, a crazy Dutch guy known as 'Bakki'. I could tell we were going to get on well as a house.

We trained that night at the club and the next night, on the Wednesday, we played a warm-up game against a touring side from Pakistan. After the game I was presented with a stick from the opposition, for being an Irish International. A lovely touch from a lovely team.

The next day, the 22nd of August, I had 2 tickets to the European Championships, to watch Ireland v England. I brought Luke as we were already great friends. Ireland lost 2:1 which meant they had a must win match v Wales. That game was two days later, and Ireland needed to win to retain 'A'

Division status. I went to watch with Luke and Ireland lost 4:0, an absolute thrashing, meaning Ireland were relegated to the 'B' Division for the tournament in two years' time.

The second week there was a hockey coaching camp on for the kids in the club, which I coached at as part of my contract. I coached Monday to Wednesday and took Thursday and Friday off as I was shattered. I didn't want to be tired for the weekend of training. I needed to make a good impression with the coach, Gilles, another Dutch man.

I had a ticket for the European Championships final, Belgium v Spain. I sat with the Irish guys, the mood was low, understandably. The home side, Belgium, thrashed Spain, 5:0.

Tobias Walter, or Tobi as he is known, a German International goalkeeper, also played for 'The Dragons'. I knew him from playing against him at international and club level when I was in Germany playing for Crefelder HTC. He lived around the corner from the 'hockey house' with his girlfriend, Annabelle, who also was playing for KHC Dragons. We went for dinner one night, just down the street at a lovely little outdoor restaurant. We chatted mainly about hockey, the matches we had against each other, the matches that were close and the matches that weren't so close. I tried speaking some of my bad German to them, they laughed. I was lucky during my time in Germany that the majority of German people spoke such good English, since they learn it from the age of 5. I could tell we would form a good friendship, in my time at KHC Dragons.

I received a text from Gilles on Thursday 29th. He wanted to meet me at the club with another man, Gregory, who I had dealt with for my pre-contract. I didn't have a good feeling about this meeting.

I drove to the club and walked to the clubhouse. I could

see Gilles sitting outside at the far end of the clubhouse. I grabbed a coffee from the bar and went to join him and Gregory. "Matthew, this isn't going to work out," Gilles said. "We were expecting a higher calibre of player from the video footage of you that we have watched, and from the things Shane said to us about you." I was stunned but, I didn't have anything to counter argue with. I couldn't say anything to change their mind. "We are giving you time to get back in contact with your old club in Germany, to see if they will re-sign you for the upcoming season." I was speechless, but I couldn't disagree with their decision. I was nowhere near the standard needed to play for one of the best clubs in Europe. I stood up, shook their hands and thanked them for the opportunity. I walked back to my car and rang my old coach from Crefelder HTC, Robin, to explain the situation, and ask if they would take me back for the upcoming season. Why should' they take me back? I turned my back on them at the end of the previous season to move to KHC Dragons. They owed me nothing. Thankfully, Robin said he would love to have me back. He knew my qualities, he knew I was a good player, and having played for Crefelder HTC for the two seasons previous, he knew what I offered and what I could bring to the team.

I rang Michael Robson, or 'Robbo' as we called him, one of my best friends in the Irish team and also a flatmate from Crefelder to explain the situation, and to say I was coming back to play for Crefelder HTC.

The next morning, Friday 30th August, Luke drove me to Eindhoven, to meet Robbo and Neal Glassey, another great friend from the Irish team, or 'Builder' as he was known, to drive me back to Krefeld. We met at a service station off the motorway, I threw my bags into the car, I hugged Luke goodbye and off we went.

With a player from the touring side from Pakistan

Time in Germany

The first week I arrived in Germany, we trained the Tuesday, Wednesday and Thursday night. We went to 'Markthalle' on the Thursday afternoon, as we did every week. Markthalle was a shopping complex which had a few different places to eat. You could get anything. Sushi, pizza, pasta. You could get also something from the butcher and have it cooked for you or have typical German food such as schnitzel.

Saturday 7th September we were in Berlin for a preseason match. A game against top side BHC, Berliner Hockey Club. I wasn't playing as I had just arrived in Germany. It wouldn't be fair for me to just 'jump' straight back into the team that I had left the previous season. It wouldn't be fair on the players that were vying for the same position as me.

After the game, as always, the home team would provide food and beer for the away team, this was due to the fact that in Germany the away team usually had quite a distance to travel. For example, Berlin was a 6-hour train journey to Düsseldorf, and then a 20-minute train to Krefeld. I let the teams go ahead of me as I didn't play. When it was my turn to get my food, I stood up and walked over to the food table. I got really dizzy, so dizzy, I fell on to the table. It collapsed. Dan Kyriakides, known as DK, a teammate who played for the Welsh national team, picked me up and put me into a chair while asking was I okay. Perdita, my manager, came over to see if everything was okay. "Are you okay Matty?" she asked. "Yeah, just give me 5 minutes, I'm still a bit dizzy." I replied. What was happening? I didn't eat my lunch. I was no longer hungry. After 5 more minutes, the dizziness passed, everything was back to normal. That was scary. It scared me and my teammates. The look of shock on their faces, said it all.

We played a pre-season match against Rot Weiss Köln, probably the best team in the German league, at their ground in Cologne on the Wednesday night. Again, I had to take myself off due to my eyesight. It was really beginning to get on my nerves. Why didn't the contacts settle in my eyes? I knew a lot of guys and girls who wore contact lenses when playing hockey and other sports, but why were mine not working?

On the Thursday, I was going out for lunch with some of my flatmates and teammates. Builder, Robbo, Niklas (the captain of our team, a German International and whose father owned and ran the club), DK and Linus (our manager Perdita's son). We went to Markthalle again as it was Thursday. Builder, Robbo and I arrived together, as we lived and travelled together. We parked up, we usually met the others inside at the tables. I opened the car door and got out. I started to feel dizzy again. I grabbed on to the car for support, I didn't want to fall over again. The guys rushed round and helped me back into the car. I sat for 5 minutes again, until the dizziness passed. When it passed, we went inside and had lunch and coffee as normal, with the rest of the guys.

When we got home, I rang Perdita. Her husband Klaus was a doctor. I explained what had happened, that I had another dizzy spell. She said she would sort something and not to drive in the meantime, just in case I had a spell while behind the wheel. That could have been fatal.

She rang me back later in the day to say that Klaus had organised an MRI scan for me the next morning. For Friday the 13th. I was to go the next day and then go to Perdita's house after, to let them know of the results.

FRIDAY THE 13TH

My other flatmate, Matthew Nelson, another Irish guy who we called 'Nelly' drove me to my appointment. I went in while Nelly sat in the car. They took me for my MRI scan and after I had to wait for a while for the results. They called me into a separate room after my scan to give me the results. For some reason I wasn't nervous, I didn't know what was coming.

"You have a brain tumour, the size of 3 golf balls in your mid brain," they said. "Sorry, what?!" I exclaimed. "You have a brain tumour, the size of three golf balls in your mid brain" they repeated. "You have to go to hospital as soon as possible because you need the pressure in your head relieved, the tumour needs to be removed as you are very close to having a brain haemorrhage."

I couldn't believe it. Me? A fit, healthy, professional hockey player. How could it be? A brain tumour? I left, in absolute shock. Walked back to the car and got in beside Nelly. I didn't say anything to him. I just took my phone out and rang Robbo. He answered and I asked to be put on speaker phone. "Guys, I'm on my way to Perdita's. She has to take me to hospital, I have a brain tumour and I need surgery as soon as possible. Got to go as need to ring my parents and Lauren." I hung up.

I rang my parents, they knew about the dizzy spells, but they didn't know I was going for the MRI. Mum answered. "Hello, Matthew, how are you?" she asked. "Are you with dad?" I asked. "Yes, why?" she replied, puzzled. "Put me on speaker phone please, I have some news to tell you." I could hear her rustling with her phone, trying to find the right button. "Okay, what do you need to tell us? Dad is here now." I didn't know how to tell them. "I'm just back from an MRI scan and they told me I have a brain tumour, the size of 3 golf balls in my mid brain. Perdita is going to take me to hospital as I need emergency surgery as soon as possible, or I'll have a brain haemorrhage. I have to go now because I'm at Perdita's but book the soonest flight to Düsseldorf that you can, I'll send you Robbo's number and he can pick you up from the airport and bring you to the hospital." I hung up. I didn't have time to sit and have a conversation with them, but I can't imagine the feelings and thoughts going through their head.

I rang Lauren and had the same conversation with her. She was on the bus to Dublin to meet her friends for a weekend together. I told her not to worry and to keep the plans she had made. I told her to go on her weekend away and I would see her soon. She didn't listen, she rang my parents about getting to Germany. When the bus stopped in Dublin, she got on a return bus as soon as possible, back to Banbridge.

I went into Perdita's. I told her what had happened, the awful news, and that she had to take me to the hospital in Duisburg, a neighbouring city to Krefeld.

We got into the car, and I rang Robbo to say we were on our way to the hospital. I asked him to pack a bag for me with clothes, underwear and my laptop. I didn't know how long I was going to be in hospital for. Robbo met us at the hospital and came in with us and waited for me to be admitted.

Hospital in Germany

I was finally admitted to hospital. Robbo set up my laptop, connected it to the Wi-Fi and we watched 'The Ashes'. We both loved watching cricket and would play on a daily basis, out our back garden, with a tennis ball and hockey stick as the bat and ball. Perdita then got me a takeaway pizza from a close by establishment as the food in the hospital wasn't anything spectacular.

I was then taken to an operating room as they needed to insert a drain into my head to relieve some of the fluid and pressure that had built up. After this was inserted I facetimed my parents to chat. I don't know what was going through their heads, seeing their only son, lying in a hospital bed, in a foreign country, with a drain sticking out of his head.

I told them to pack for one week after speaking to Prof. Scholz who was performing the operation, because I would be allowed out of hospital after my surgery, or so we thought. It turned out to be 6 weeks.

Jens Westphal, a father of one of the players in the team, asked would Professor Scholz, a family friend, perform my surgery. Jens worked in another hospital as the Head of Urology and Paediatric Urology.

Prof. Scholz is renowned as one of the best neurosurgeons in Germany, if not the world. People in Dubai and the UAE pay for him to fly out to perform their neurosurgeries, which shows how highly regarded he is. Jens asked him to perform my surgery as a favour to him and the club, thankfully, he agreed. What a bit of luck that one of the best neurosurgeons in Germany was going to operate on me. The first bit of good luck in a long time.

Mum, Dad and Lauren arrived in Düsseldorf the next morning. Robbo picked them up at the airport and drove them straight to the hospital in Duisburg.

My parents and Lauren arrived at the hospital 10 minutes after I had been taken to theatre. They went up to my ward and asked where I was, but they said I had been taken for my operation. My initial surgery was 7 hours long, in a seated position, so they could access the tumour and visiting was over by the time they had finished with me. My parents and Lauren couldn't see me till the next morning, when visiting hours started again. My parents didn't sleep the Friday night, or the Saturday night, after I broke them the news of my tumour. 48 hours of hell for them. I can't imagine what was going through their heads. The thoughts and feelings that they would have experienced.

Prof. Scholz managed to remove 90% of the tumour, the last 10% was deemed in too dangerous an area to attempt to remove. He could have paralysed me, or even worse, killed me.

After my initial surgery, I was in Intensive Care for 4 weeks. 1 week on Prof. Scholz's private ward and then 1 week in a high dependency unit, as my health had deteriorated. I stopped eating and talking in that last week of hospital in Germany. I refused all food and had to be fed through a tube into the side of my neck and through my nose, with some kind of cocktail of blended up ingredients.

Also, after my first surgery, on recommendation from Prof. Scholz, I was to wear an eyepatch on alternating eyes every day, as my eyesight had been affected before and after surgery. I had double vision, I could tell what the real image was, but there was a shadow directly beside the proper image, of the same thing. I had to wear the patch to retrain my eyes, to get them back to normal.

Lauren went home after one week as she had to go back to work as a physiotherapist, but we had a facetime call most nights. I also called my sister Ashlea, and my brother-in-law Timmy, most days as well. They were unable to come to Germany as they were both working.

On the 19th of September, at 3am, I rang my mum, twice. Of course, she didn't pick up. It was 3am after all. I left her a voicemail, asking her to come pick me up from my house, and to bring me T-shirts, as I didn't have any clean ones left. The medication I was on had made me delirious.

In my time in Germany, I had a total of 5 surgeries, to introduce drains, to alleviate pressure, as the fluid in my brain wasn't draining away by itself down into my abdomen, the way it should have been. These drains couldn't stay in permanently, so they introduced a programmable shunt, and then a second one because the first wasn't doing the job. They worked and are still in my head today and will stay there, as trying to take them out would cause more damage, than good.

I also had to have a catheter inserted during my time in Germany. I couldn't regulate when I needed to urinate. I kept waking up with soaking wet pyjamas bottoms. It would stay with me for 16 weeks. Also introduced, were my 'adult nappies', as I called them. Apart from not knowing when I needed to urinate, I also didn't know when I needed to defecate. I was doubly incontinent. The nappies stayed with me for a long time too. 26 and being doubly incontinent, what had happened to me.

My tumour was sent off to somewhere else in Germany to be tested. The results came back on the 24th of September saying it was 3% cancer. There was a small speck, somewhere in the tumour, that showed up as cancer. 3% is nothing, but since they didn't remove all the tumour, it meant I would have to go back to Northern Ireland for cancer treatment, whatever that might entail.

I was visited on a daily basis by teammates, coaching staff, friends I had made outside of hockey, every day for the 6 weeks I was in hospital. I couldn't be more grateful. They looked after me so well, bringing me food and a bit of banter, to put a smile on my face. It gave my dad great entertainment to see how much Builder despised hospitals. He hated them, hated everything about them but he still came to see me, which shows what a great friend he is.

I recently found out that every Thursday I spent in hospital in Germany, the same guys, especially Niklas, came to see me with buns from Markthalle. He said that since I couldn't go to Markthalle with the guys, they would bring Markthalle to me. This shows how incredible my teammates and friends are.

It was my dad's birthday on the 17th of October. I'm sure it's a birthday he will never forget. Watching his only son lie in a hospital bed, with a lot of tubes and machines stuck to me, bleeping away. The early hours of the 18th I was taken for emergency surgery. It was at this point I took a turn for the worst. I couldn't be woken, there was no response from me to anything. They took me for a CT scan, and this showed that my shunt had blocked, so they needed to drain away the fluid from my brain and introduce a second shunt. My parents didn't sleep that night. Dad rang the hospital at 3am to check on me and he was told that a second shunt had been introduced and it seemed to be helping.

At this point, I stopped talking. I wouldn't utter a word, and I don't know why. I wouldn't speak until I arrived at the Royal Victoria Hospital, Belfast.

We had no idea how I was getting home from Germany, back to hospital in Northern Ireland. Prof. Scholz said I wasn't well enough to go on a commercial flight. Dad planned out a route for driving. He would take a rental car from Duisburg, to the channel tunnel, drive to England, take a ferry across to Ireland and then drive me to hospital in Belfast.

Thankfully, one of my mum's oldest and closest friends came to the rescue, Joan Wells. Joan had a senior role within the Belfast Trust. She was co-director of maternity services. She organised an air ambulance from Woodgate Aviation, to take me home from Düsseldorf to the airport in Antrim.

Joan and my mum's other best friend, Jackie Stewart, came to Germany. Joan had to finalise the air ambulance details from the side in Germany. Jackie came along for moral support for my mum, and my family. They stayed 4 days and left the day before our departure.

I flew home on the 28th of October, with my dad in the air ambulance, and a nurse on board to look after me. We nearly had to touch down in Liverpool as my vitals were slightly concerning, but thankfully they persevered on and landed in Antrim. I was then 'blue lighted' by ambulance straight to the Royal Victoria Hospital in Belfast with my dad in the ambulance, to be met by my mum, sister, brother-in-law, Lauren and Joan. She came across as she was working in the hospital.

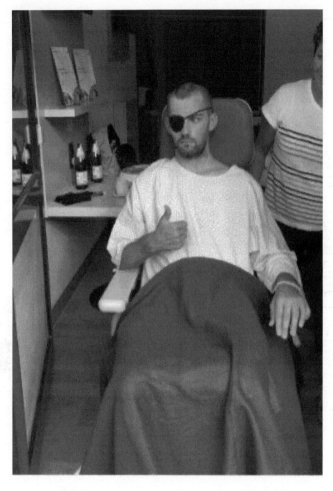

In my hospital room in Germany with my eyepatch

Matthew Bell

Mum, Dad and I outside the hospital in Germany

Jackie, Myself and Joan

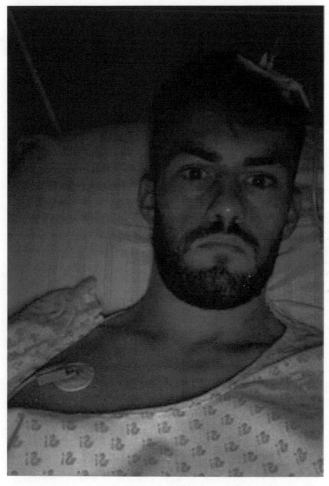

*Me with the drain in my head, this is the image my parents would
have seen on our first FaceTime*

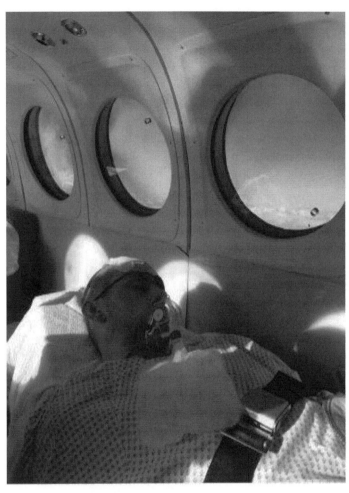

Sleeping in the air ambulance on the way back to NI

ROYAL VICTORIA HOSPITAL

I was admitted to the Royal Victoria Hospital (RVH) in Belfast for 3 weeks of tests. I was under the care of Mr. Weir, a consultant neurologist.

When I was admitted, I spoke to dad once, the only words I would say for a long time. "I need to pee, dad" I said. "I really need to pee." That was it, my days of speaking were over. Was I to be voiceless for the rest of my life?

My catheter had blocked on the flight, the change in air pressure had caused it. They had to change my catheter, to make me more comfortable. When they removed the initial catheter, my urine went everywhere, and I couldn't stop it. It was a horrible mess, and highly embarrassing but there was nothing I could do to stop it.

Mr. Weir told my parents he wasn't sure if I'd ever walk or talk again or if I would get my volition back - (be able to cut up my own food, feed myself) things like that. I was in a more unstable condition than he had anticipated. He had read my notes and spoken with Prof. Scholz but hadn't expected me to be so poorly, I was in an awful state. How had I gone from being a fulltime, professional sportsperson, to not eating or even speaking? I wouldn't make a sound. I was a complete vegetable, or as Sheena MacAuley – one of my closest female friends had renamed me a 'parsnip', because apparently that's a cute vegetable.

The 28th and 29th of October were the dates of the Olympic qualifier matches that the Irish men's team were to play in. Matches that I would probably have been playing in, if I wasn't in hospital. They were to play Canada, in Canada. The reason for this was Canada were ranked higher than Ireland in the world rankings. Ireland won the first game 5-3 and lost the second game 3-1. The aggregate score was 6-6 which meant the tie was to go to shootouts. Ireland lost on shootouts which meant they didn't qualify for the Tokyo 2020 Olympics. Dad came into my hospital room to tell me they hadn't qualified. I wasn't speaking, so I didn't respond.

I had to be fed through my neck and nose for the final 2 weeks in Germany. In Belfast I had to have a Percutaneous Endoscopic Gastrostomy tube inserted (a PEG tube, as it was known), a feeding tube placed directly into my stomach. Why wasn't I eating? Back when I was playing hockey I ate like a horse. Anything and everything around me, in large quantities. The PEG tube would stay with me, even when I started eating again, as they fed me through it overnight to build me back up to my original weight.

I also wasn't able to swallow my own saliva. I had lost the power to swallow. I was introduced to a small suction machine. The nurse would turn the machine on and would use the straw like nozzle to suck up the saliva that had pooled in my mouth, my cheeks and under my tongue. This became routine, every couple of hours, the nurse or nursing assistant would come in to drain my mouth out.

All my medication had to be given intravenously and the nurses had to use a sponge to dampen my tongue and lips. After removing the saliva with the vacuum, my mouth was very dry. It was a constant rotation of sucking out the saliva and dampening my mouth.

Since I wasn't speaking, the NHS staff decided to introduce a way for me to communicate on a 'yes' or 'no' basis. My speech and language therapists introduced a big red button for me to press. I would press the button once for 'yes' or press it twice for 'no'. I had to be asked very direct questions. If you asked me a question that needed an explanation, as an answer, you would get a 'yes' or 'no' in response.

It eventually progressed onto laminated sheets of paper, with different words on it, and I would point to whatever word that would correlate with the question asked. The reason for this was that some people didn't know when I had pressed the button, as it didn't make a noise, apart from the button hitting the casing.

I don't have many memories from my time in the RVH. The only memory I really have is the day my mum came into my room to cut my fingernails. I had very sharp nail clippers in my washbag that my mum used. She completed my right hand, then moved onto my left. When she got to the last finger, my little finger, her hand slipped, or something distracted her, and she clipped my finger and not the nail. It started to bleed, heavily. Mum ran out to find a nurse. They thought it might need a stitch, it was so deep. Thankfully it didn't come to that, and the nurse just heavily strapped it. Every time mum clipped my fingernails and toenails after this, I had a slight fear she would do it again.

On Sunday 17th November all tests had been carried out and my 2 week isolation period had finished (when you are transferred in from a hospital outside of the UK you must remain in isolation for two weeks). I was transferred to the City Hospital, to The Cancer Centre, to start my cancer treatment. Along with Tori Mills and Sheena MacAuley, two of my closest friends, Ashlea my sister and Lauren, they followed the ambulance to the City hospital and saw me into my private room.

BELFAST CITY HOSPITAL

I arrived in the City Hospital to undergo 12 weeks of chemotherapy with oncologist Olabode Oladipo (he was known as Bode, pronounced Bode-ee). I still wasn't speaking or eating.

One of the nurses, Mandy, an older nurse, with blue hair, said to my sister, "That man will dance out of this hospital". I don't know why she said it, but it stuck with my sister, and my parents. They were thinking 'yeah, right'. Me? Someone who wasn't well enough to walk, talk, or eat for myself? Not a chance I would dance out of that hospital.

The speech and language therapists in The Cancer Centre, changed my conversing techniques. Anytime I would lift my arm to point to a word on the page, for some reason, my arm would stay in the same position. It was rigid. I couldn't bring it back to my side by myself, I needed someone to lower it for me. If I had an itch on my nose I would scratch it and then need a nurse, my parents, sister, Lauren or my friends to move my arm back down to my side. They changed the way I would answer 'yes' or 'no'. The person talking to me, would take my hand and I would squeeze once for yes, and twice for no. Just like the big button, but this time they would know if I had squeezed.

I had to have a Peripherally Inserted Central Catheter (PICC) line inserted into my right arm to administer the chemotherapy drugs to my bloodstream. They also used the PICC line to take blood samples. I kept it in when my treatment finished because they had to keep checking my bloods, and I hated needles. Strange to think, after everything I had been through to this point, that I still hated the sight and feeling of needles, but no one likes needles, right?

I started my chemotherapy treatment on the 19th of November. It was deemed a very 'heavy' regime. 12 weeks of treatment, 1 week of the chemotherapy drug entering my body, 24 hours a day then 2 weeks off, to allow my blood count to regulate. I can still picture the nurses bringing that trolley into my room, with the squeaky wheels, to hang that black bag beside my bed, connect it to my PICC line, and allow the toxic substances to enter my body. I don't think I'll ever forget that image till the day I die.

One day, when I wasn't connected up to my chemotherapy, I was taken down to a set of scales just down the corridor from my room to see what weight I was after weeks of not eating. I weighed in at 55kg. 23kg less than my normal body weight. My clothes were wearing me.

I was bedridden. So immobile that I couldn't get out of bed without the help of the nursing staff and my wheelchair. I had to brush my teeth in the bed, with a cardboard dish to spit the toothpaste into. I would then rinse my mouth with some water and spit again. The nurses would dispose of the dish and take my toothbrush off me. I had to have bed baths because I couldn't have a shower. The nurses would come in and wash me by hand with a basin of warm, soapy water and paper towels.

Once the catheter had been removed and a couple of weeks spent toilet training me like a two year old I was able to use a bedside bottle that slotted into the side of my bed for ease of access. I would roll on to one side, pee into it and then one of the nurses would empty it into the toilet. When I needed to do my other business, I had to be wheeled into my bathroom, where the toilet had a raised seat, with handles for me to hold on to. I was helped to lower my trousers and boxers and then helped onto the raised seat. I was then left alone, the door would be closed behind me. I would do my business and then I would ring the buzzer beside the toilet to let a nurse or nursing assistant know I had finished. They would then wipe me down, help me get my boxers and pyjama bottoms back on and help me back into my wheelchair, wheel me back to the side of my bed, then help me out of the chair and into my bed. I really was a vegetable, or a parsnip.

My grandparents, my mum's parents hadn't been allowed to come see me. My mum wouldn't allow them because I was so ill, she didn't want them to see me in such a state. Both of them have had cancer, so they were familiar with The Cancer Centre. My nanny, Betty, had previously had breast cancer, which just required surgery and then approximately twenty years later developed lung cancer where she had radiotherapy to finish her treatment. That was my first experience of The Cancer Centre, when I drove her up for one of her radiotherapy appointments. Little did I know, a few years later, I would be back for my own treatment. My papa, Sydney, also had cancer, kidney cancer, which was removed by surgery. Our family's lives, like the majority of families lives, have been affected by cancer. It's a scary statistic that one in two people, 50% of us, will someday have cancer.

One morning, I ventured into my bathroom, with the help of a nurse in my wheelchair to wash my face for myself and brush my teeth. I looked in the mirror. There wasn't a hair on my body, not even an eyelash. I looked ill, very ill. I looked like a cancer patient, I was a cancer patient. That was the first time I had seen myself in a mirror since losing all of my hair and it's an image that I will never forget..

I wasn't sick once during my chemotherapy treatment. It was unheard of. Bode said I was the only patient ever, under his care, to go through that kind of chemotherapy regime, and not be sick once. He said the reason I wasn't sick, was due to my high level of fitness, being a professional and international sportsperson.

One day, dad walked into my room, and I could tell he had something on his mind. The look on his face said there was something bugging him. He pulled up a chair beside my bed and looked me in the eyes.

"We need to talk about something," he said sternly.

"I know you can speak. You know you can speak, so pull your finger out and start speaking!" He sat and lectured me for another ten minutes before putting the chair back, getting up and leaving the room.

Later that same day, Ashlea and Timmy came to visit me. I whispered a very faint 'yes' or 'no' to them after they spoke to me. That was the start of it. Dad's lecture had worked. That was the start of me beginning to talk again.

The next morning the nurses came in to take a blood sample and I spoke to them. I was later told they went outside the room and cried, telling everyone 'he's speaking again!'. I know this may make the nurses and NHS staff seem 'weak', but I think it shows how much their job means to them, it shows how much they care. They really don't get the recognition they deserve for what they do and how they treat every patient the same. As if each patient was a family member of their own.

The first time my grandparents came to see me was a Sunday morning in December. Dad drove them down and they got to see me for the first time in four months. I'm sure they were shocked at how I looked, but they certainly didn't show it. After that they took the train from Lurgan weekly, where they lived. To the stop outside The City Hospital, and then walked from the train station to the hospital. All I can remember from one of these visits was my nanny came into the room and put her hand on my foot. "Nanny, your hands are cold!" I exclaimed. She also had brought me an iced finger, from a bakery in Lurgan that I loved. She did this the first time she came to see me, and every time after.

I had to practice getting in and out of a car because I was so immobile. As I continued to improve, Nicola, my OT thought it would benefit me to get out of hospital for short trips to go for coffee, lunches and some fresh air. This was the start of my rehabilitation back into society and the planning for eventually moving home. In the middle of December, Nicola, had to help with this. Dad would park the car out the back of the hospital. I would be wheeled out in my wheelchair to the side of the car, helped out of my wheelchair and I would reverse myself into the car, backside first, my legs were then helped into the car and the door closed for me. I then had to be helped out of the car, I could barely support my own weight. I needed one, if not two people to help me back into my wheelchair.

A couple of days later was the first time I went to 'Chat' coffee shop. This was the coffee shop in the reception of The Cancer Centre. Mum and dad came up to my room and helped me into my wheelchair and wheeled me to the lifts, then over to the coffee shop. They removed a chair from one of the tables so I could sit at the table. Ashlea drove up to visit that day as well. I was very uneasy as this was my first time out of a hospital ward since September. I was very nervous and self-conscious with how I looked to the public. I never used to be self-conscious. I didn't care what people thought of me. This time was different because I looked like a cancer patient. I had no hair, I was skinny and in a wheelchair. This was my first coffee since Germany. I used to love coffee. When I was in Germany playing, I would have drunk 4 or 5 cups a day, to get me through all the training and matches. We finished our drinks and treats. I had gulped down my coffee and I then asked to be taken back to my room, I wanted back in my bed, away from the public eye. Happy to be out of view.

My first day trip out of hospital was on the 22nd of December, we went to 'Loughshore Carpark' in Jordanstown. Jordanstown was a very familiar area to me. This was where I had my gym sessions each week for the Irish team, in the university, at the Sports Institute of Northern Ireland, or 'SINI', for short. My parents, Lauren and I went. We arrived and my wheelchair was removed from the car, I was helped into it and my dad started to push me. Being a physio, Lauren wanted to get me walking. So, with the help of my parents and Lauren, they helped me out of the chair, and on to my feet. Lauren put her arm around me and held one of my hands for support as my balance was still appalling. We walked for maybe 50 metres before I wanted back in my wheelchair. After the walk, we all went to McDonalds for lunch. 50m isn't very much, but to me it meant the world.

In the hospital, I had been practising with cutlery, and by cutlery, I meant a plastic baby spoon and a yellow baby bowl. The bowl had a special lip to help the food on to my spoon. I was literally a baby, in an adult's body. I would have to relearn a lot of things in my time in hospital. Things that are simple to all adults, except to me, they were very difficult.

'The Ramada Hotel', at Shaw's Bridge in Belfast was the location of my next big outing, after Christmas Day. I went for a lunch with my parents on the 29th of December. I had a steak sandwich, chips and pepper sauce. I loved steak. My favourite meal. This was the first time I used a fork by myself, I just picked it up without thinking. Mum had to cut my steak sandwich for me, but I ate everything on my plate. That was the first time I had used a fork since I had been in hospital, over 4 months.

That was the start of it, my rehab. Even though I had been doing weekly work, with my OT, Nicola, my archnemesis, that was the first sign of normality resuming. I say Nicola was my archnemesis, but she was the one who pushed me, when I needed pushing. She kicked me into gear, when I wasn't feeling up to it. She would drag me out of my bed, which was a rarity, when I needed dragging. She could see the potential in me, when no one else did, and without her stubbornness and constant care, I wouldn't be where I am today. So, I have to say a massive thank you to her, for being so stubborn with me, which is just what I needed.

When I was back to my normal eating habits there is one day of eating, that I remember vividly. I had my hospital lunch given to me and my parents also brought me a boojum when they came to visit me an hour after I had already eaten. They left after an hour since I had a visitor coming to see me, an Irish hockey teammate of mine, Sean Murray. Sean had texted me before he came to say he was stopping at McDonald's and asked if I wanted anything; I told him I'd take a 'wrap of the day', small fries and a drink. He arrived just before my parents left and they couldn't believe their eyes. Another meal for me, my third lunch. I was really making up for my 7 weeks of not eating.

I also had to practise going up and down the stairs. My balance was still far from normal. I had to walk up two feet on each step at a time, while holding on to the bannister with one hand and using a crutch in my other hand, for support.

Just before Christmas, my friendship group, which we called 'Camel', came to visit me in hospital. Those that were in the country. Every year, for nine years we have had a Christmas dinner at Rachael's house, where everyone brought something for the dinner. A mix of finger food for nibbles, Dermy's infamous vegetable soup, as a starter, which we thought was homemade, until recently, the secret was out that it was actually bought from a butchers in Banbridge. Turkey, ham, vegetables, roast potatoes and gravy, for the main course. Mum always made one of the desserts, usually a cheesecake, and someone else would make another, plus wine, lots of wine, but this year was obviously very different.

Instead of doing a Christmas dinner, 'Camel' came to my room to do a Secret Santa. Most of the group came, plus Chris, an English guy who we had befriended at university in Belfast. We had a great evening, the craic was flowing, and presents were exchanged. I can't thank my friends enough, for everything that they have done for me, since my diagnosis and admittance to hospital in Belfast. I hope I can repay the kindness they showed me, somehow, if that's even possible.

That night must have taken a lot out of me because I pressed my buzzer to get the nurses attention. Nurse Lauren came in and asked everyone to leave the room so she could see what was up with me. I told her I was shattered and wanted to go to bed. So, she wheeled me into the bathroom and got me ready for bed and then allowed everyone back into my room to see me before she asked them to politely leave.

When I was mobile enough to have a shower, the bed baths stopped. A nursing assistant, Jim, would help with this. I would be wheeled into the bathroom and helped to take my clothes off. I was then transferred over to a seat beside the shower. Jim would start the shower and then cover me in water. He would then have to apply shower gel to my body and head, my bald head. I was mobile enough to have a shower but not mobile enough to wash myself, I still had a long way to go before normality resumed in my life.

After I was showered, I had to be dried. I still needed help drying myself. Jim would dry me down and help me into clothes as I wasn't able to even put my arms into a t-shirt. I would eventually move on to being able to dry my head and the front of my torso, but I would need help with the rest of my body.

To work on my speech, I had a speech and language

therapist called Aileen. She would work with me on a weekly basis and would make me practise my vowels. I would have to sound out my a's, e's and o's. as I said, a baby in an adult's body.

When I needed to go to the toilet, I would use my buzzer to get the attention of one of the nurses or I would shout for nurse Lauren, as the nurse's station was just outside of my room and the door was always open. It was a rarity when I used the buzzer because I was checked on so often by the wonderful NHS staff.

First time in 'Chat' coffee shop with my parents. You can see the PEG tube under my t-shirt.

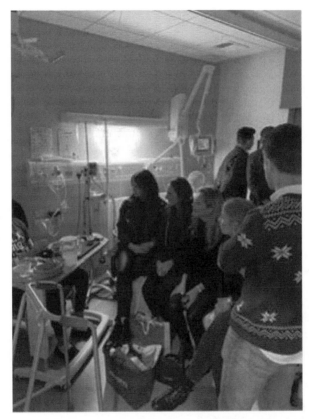

All my best friends in my hospital room for Secret Santa

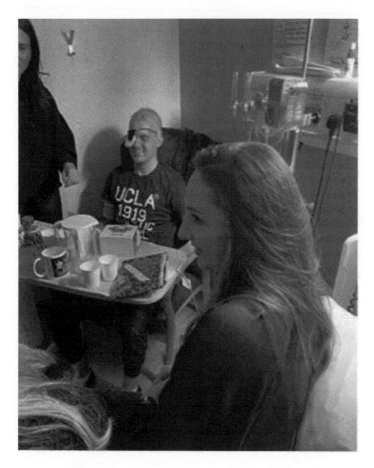

Me sitting in the corner of my room during Secret Santa

Me and Josh, when my team from Germany came to Ireland for a preseason match v my old club Banbridge HC

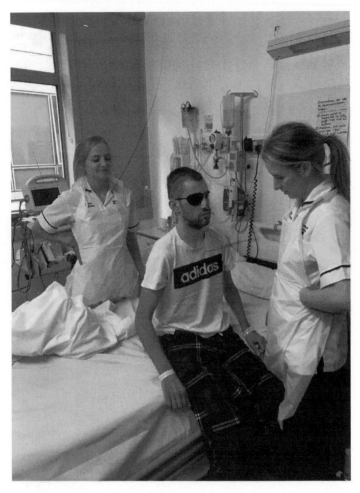

This photo shows ho skinny I was at my lightest weight of 55kg

CHRISTMAS DAY 2019

Another morning, waking up in my hospital bed. Everything was the same, except the nurses who came in to check my bloods had massive smiles on their faces, bigger than usual. They always had a smile on their face, which made my hospital experience a lot easier than it could have been. "Happy Christmas Matthew" they exclaimed. I replied with a "Happy Christmas" back to them. It wasn't a normal Christmas, who wants to spend Christmas in hospital?

Tori came to see me that morning, dressed as an elf, with a sack full of presents. She didn't want me to be alone on Christmas morning. This shows how amazing my friends are, I couldn't be more grateful to them all, for everything but especially, the support in the worst year of my life.

I had Christmas dinner in hospital at lunchtime, placed in front of me on a tray, with the yellow kids' bowl. I still wasn't eating off a normal plate in hospital. Turkey, ham, pigs in blankets, stuffing, a roast potato, a large spoonful of mash, carrots and sprouts, my most hated vegetable, and a large helping of gravy. I ate it all, apart from the sprouts.

Ruth came to visit me when my lunch was placed in front of me around midday. She watched me eat it and we chatted about a few things. Mainly how I was excited about going to Ashlea's house for Christmas dinner. I also mentioned that I wasn't sure how good a cook Ashlea was, but I never should have doubted her. Ruth later told me she cried when she left my room walking down the corridor to the exit. After she left, I had sent her a text message saying thanks for coming, with a heart emoji. She cried at that message, too. That was the first time I had texted her since everything had happened and it made her emotional.

My parents came to pick me up that afternoon. I was going home, kind of. I was to go to my sister, Ashlea's house. Timmy, her husband and Ash, as I called her, were making Christmas dinner. My second Christmas dinner of the day, the only positive to come from still being in hospital. I was rolled into the house, in my wheelchair and helped out by my mum and dad, into the sofa. When it was dinner time, I was rolled into the kitchen and I sat at the end of the table, still in my wheelchair.

They did an amazing job. Kudos to them for making their first Christmas dinner so well. Again, I finished everything on my plate and thankfully there were no sprouts to be seen.

Ash, Timmy, my parents and my mum's parents, Sydney and Betty, were there for dinner and then Lauren came around after to visit, to wish everyone a happy Christmas. Lauren and I just lay up on the sofa, watching TV and eating dessert. Ash had prepared a white chocolate cheesecake, one of my favourite desserts.

I had a plastic bag brought with me to Ashlea's house. This was filled with things I needed from hospital, including my medication and adult nappies. My parents asked me every half an hour or so, if I needed to go to the toilet, or they sent me there every hour as I still didn't know when I needed to do my business.

Before I knew it, it was time to go back to hospital. So, we packed everything we had up, my parents wheeled me out to the car, and I was helped into the front seat, to be taken back. I was sad, I could sense normality was resuming, I had a wonderful day, with a lot of eating, that I didn't want to end but I had to be back in hospital for 20:30. We got in the car, drove back to Belfast and my dad wheeled me into my room and helped me into my bed. This was my new normal, which I didn't like.

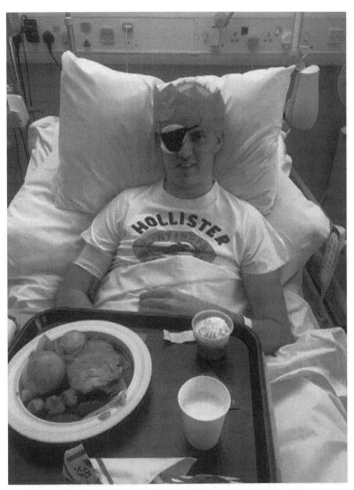

*Me in my hospital bed with my first Christmas dinner of the day.
Notice the yellow baby plate.*

Tori in her elf costume that she wore to visit me

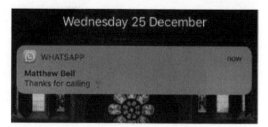

The message I sent Ruth after she left my room

Leaving Hospital

I finished my chemotherapy regime near the end of January 2020. The first part of my treatment was over, after surgery. I just had radiotherapy to go through. Luckily, I would be allowed to travel from home to my radiotherapy appointments and didn't have to be an inpatient. I wasn't allowed to leave hospital straight away, since chemotherapy affected your blood count, I had to stay in hospital until my blood count normalised, but I got to ring the bell. Not the bell on the wall in the corridor, I was too immobile to go to it, so they brought me a handheld bell to ring from my bed. My mum and dad came to witness me ringing the bell.

At this stage I was no longer using my wheelchair. I had progressed on to a rollator. Something you see an elderly person using around your local shop. The only difference is mine didn't have a shopping bag in the middle. I would use this to help me walk. A 3 wheeled device with brakes on it in case I started to lose control.

I was allowed home at the start of February for a 2-night stay. This was a Saturday and Sunday night. The first time I would sleep in my own bed in over 6 months. I had to go back to hospital on the Monday morning. I was supposed to be discharged later on in the week, around the Thursday or Friday but since the weekend had gone so smoothly, and I had pestered the staff so much, I went into hospital on the Monday and was discharged on the Tuesday. Normality again was resuming. Slowly, but it was still moving in the right direction.

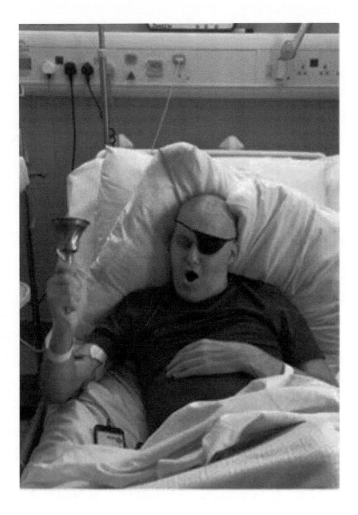

Ringing the bell after completing chemotherapy treatment

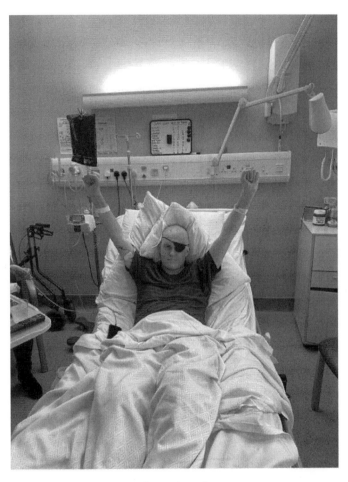

After completing chemotherapy treatment

RADIOTHERAPY

I was supposed to start my radiotherapy treatment in the middle of February. I walked into reception, with my rollator and mum at my side, after my dad had dropped us to the entrance and I told them my name. I was handed a buzzer, for when my slot was to start in one of the bays. I checked the screen to see what bay I was in, it was to be in bay 7. Dad at this point had parked the car and had joined us in the waiting room. My buzzer went off after 10 minutes of waiting, so I pushed myself out of the chair, held on to my rollator and walked to bay 7. I went in and the radiologist spoke to me, "How are you today, Matthew?". "I'm great thanks, ready to get the last part of my treatment started!" They helped me on to the bed and took my rollator away.

The way radiotherapy works is that you lie face down on a bed, put your face into a mould that has been specifically made for you, they then put the back of the mould on to your head to clamp you to the bed. You then must lie as still as possible, while the radiation machine rotates around you, or at least that is what's supposed to happen.

My mask didn't fit.

I had put on so much weight after they had taken my initial mould that the mask no longer fitted my face. The clamp wouldn't close the back of the mask on to the front. They tried for a good hour, different ways to try and make it fit, but no luck. I had to get back off the bed, go back to reception and make a new appointment for another mask to be fitted and made. This delayed my treatment by a week as they had to take a new mould of my face and have it manufactured. A new appointment was made for the following week of February, so dad had to drive me back up to The City Hospital for my second 'radiotherapy planning' to take place. That is what they called the mask making process. I had to lie on a bed, and they made a paper mache mould of the front of my face, then they did the same for the back of my head. I was then told my mask wouldn't be ready until the end of the week. My treatment would start the following Wednesday, the 26th of February.

I received 7 weeks of radiotherapy treatment. Apparently, radiotherapy would cause the remainder of my tumour to disappear. It would melt away, like a snowball on a hot plate.

It was 7 weeks of treatment, Monday to Friday, with the weekends off, which was nice. I would get a lie in at the weekends. All my treatment times were in the morning. After my treatment, I would go home and have my lunch, then make my way to the sofa for an afternoon nap of roughly 2 hours. At the weekends I was sleeping from 10:30pm to 10am, straight through, without waking once. I probably could have slept longer but my alarm woke me to take my medication, Keppra, which is an anti-seizure drug. 11.5 hours of sleep and a 2-hour nap in the afternoon, that's a lot of sleep, but my body obviously needed it. After all, they do say sleep is the best form of recovery for your body.

After day one of treatment, I came home to have lunch. I sat at the table, waiting for mum to make me my lunch. I threw up. It just happened. I didn't know it was coming, I just threw up all over the table. Mum rang the hospital and they said they would change my anti-sickness medication and the tablets could be collected the next day, when I was up for treatment. The tablets were collected the next day and I started them straight away. It happened again, for another 2 days. The same thing, sitting at the table and I just vomited. Mum rang the hospital again, so they got me steroids to go alongside the anti-sickness. I started the steroids too, and the vomiting stopped.

When I was back home, the raised toilet seat came with me. I still wasn't able to lower myself onto a normal toilet. The difference was this time I was able to clean myself down after using the toilet. I know my parents did it for me as a baby, but at the age of 26, I think that would have been a step too far.

My shower seat came home with me also. I needed the shower gel and the hair thickening shampoo set on the floor of the shower as I couldn't reach up to the rack to lift the products off. I still didn't have any hair, but I was hoping the shampoo would kick start the process.

The coronavirus pandemic hit Northern Ireland during the time of my radiotherapy treatment. One week, going into the waiting room, everything was normal. The next week, it was chaos. My parents weren't allowed in through the front door, as the hospital was closed to anyone who wasn't working or receiving treatment. There were temperature checks at the front door, from staff with facemasks on. Hand sanitizer everywhere. You weren't allowed into the hospital without sanitising your hands. The buzzers in the waiting room were gone, a member of staff would come into the waiting room, shout the patient's name for their treatment and would direct you into the bay for you to receive your treatment. Certain seats in the waiting room had laminated sheets on them, with a big 'X' so you wouldn't sit in them, to adhere to social distancing rules. Some people wore facemasks and gloves, although they weren't essential. It was weird to walk into that waiting room and see people wearing facemasks and face shields. Was the world going mad?

During the time of my radiotherapy treatment, I was working with one of the Cancer Centre's physiotherapists,

Paula, on my walking and balance. I would see her twice a week. After a couple of weeks work with her, I was off my rollator, and using a single crutch for balance and help walking. A big step on my road to recovery, and normality. She would also help me practise going up and down the stairs, too. I used my rollator for 3 weeks of my radiotherapy and eventually, Paula took it away. I was on to a single crutch. At this point, I was starting to go up the stairs more normally. One foot, for one step, rather than my usual two feet on one step, with the crutch in my right hand and using my left hand to hold the bannister.

Paula had me using the treadmill, to practise my walking, as my balance was so poor I was walking with a very wide gait. If I fell, I wouldn't be able to get back on to my feet, like a normal person could. I had somehow forgotten how to get back on to my feet. I would need something to grab on to, a piece of furniture or someone close to me would have to help me up. We did a couple of minutes walking, with me holding on to the treadmill to both handles. Eventually, after a few sessions, we moved on to running. Something I hadn't done for 6 months. It started in the corridor, a length of about 10 metres, with Paula supporting my chest with one hand and my back with her other hand. She ran beside me. We ran from the physio room, down to the window. I stumbled and nearly fell, but Paula caught me. After the first time I ran, we did this every time I had a session with Paula and eventually, we moved on to the treadmill, with me holding both handles to keep my balance. I ran for a time of 30 seconds, the furthest I had run in months. I was seriously out of breath after 30 seconds of running. I used to be a professional and international hockey player, who loved running. My fitness levels had completely reset to zero.

I was back to my normal eating routine, maybe even eating more due to the steroid medication I was on. Mum decided to watch what I was eating, I had put on a bit more weight than when I was playing hockey. When I was playing, I was 78kg, but mostly muscle. Since I had lain in a hospital bed for so long, my muscle had wasted away. I was back to 78kg, if not heavier, with very little of it the muscle I used to have. She controlled my intake of food at breakfast, lunch and dinner, to try and get me back to my normal weight.

The last week of my radiotherapy came. My parents said to me, "You're walking in and out of hospital, without that crutch, as if everything is back to normal." We had been practising 'no stick' walking around our housing development every so often but that was only for 10/20m at a time. I didn't want to, but I agreed. So I walked in and out for treatment, as if everything was back to normal, and that was another step on the road to normality, no more walking aids.

The 17th of April came. The last day of my cancer treatment. I finished my last half an hour on the bed, with that machine 'zapping' me. The machine finished, I got off the bed and thanked the members of staff that helped me in the radiotherapy treatment room and walked out. Mum and dad were allowed in to see me ring the bell. I walked down the corridor with a massive smile on my face, still very bald, as radiotherapy had stopped the growth of hairs on my body. Mum and dad were waiting for me. They stood up when I walked in, and we walked over to the bell together. I grabbed it and nearly rang it off the wall. Everyone in the waiting room clapped. I was ecstatic.

We went to 'Boojum', a favourite of mine, a burrito bar on the Lisburn Road in Belfast, for a celebratory lunch. Lauren Scott, one of my favourite nurses from 'The City Hospital', who I called 'nurse Lauren', had become a good friend. She came to congratulate me with a box of donuts, a love we both shared. We couldn't hug, due to covid restrictions. Again, this shows how above and beyond the NHS staff go for their patients.

I got home and checked my phone. I had been sent two videos, one from Josh and one from my female friends. The video from Josh was a montage of clips of hockey players and friends sending me a congratulations message for finishing my treatment. Players from the Irish team and Banbridge Hockey Club. The video from the girls was a lip sync video of the Camel girls singing 'I'll be there for you', the Friends TV show theme tune. I watched both multiple times and I started to cry. The support I'd received over my time going through treatment was overwhelming and unbelievable, how could I ever repay my friends, for the love, kindness and support they'd shown me?

I had thrown up for a couple of days in a row, at dinner time. Just before mum set my plate in front of me. I vomited all over the table, without any warning. It just hit me. I also didn't have very much of an appetite. I was barely eating anything. The radiotherapy was having a stronger effect on my body, than the chemotherapy.

Mum rang Bode's secretary to explain what had happened. They decided to bring me for a check-up, at the end of May back to The City Hospital, to get my bloods checked. The result of this check-up meant I was to go back on to my steroid tablets and for my anti-sickness tablets to be changed. Also, from this check-up, they decided to bring my first scan forward. It was supposed to be in July, but they brought it forward to the start of June.

I went to the hospital, at the start of June for my scan. I had to have an x-ray before the scan to check the levels on my shunts. My shunts are programmable shunts, and the settings can be altered by magnets. An MRI scan could change the settings. I had an x-ray before the scan to see the settings, and an x-ray after the scan to make sure the settings hadn't changed. I also had a cannula inserted to my arm, as during the scan they would insert a contrast dye into my bloodstream, to provide better clarity and decipherability to images. The scan lasted 30 minutes, halfway through, the nurse came in to inject the dye. After the scan was over, the cannula was removed, and I was allowed to go home, after my shunt settings had been checked.

Due to coronavirus, my physio with Paula had stopped. She had organised a 12-week, online PT course, with one of the Cancer Centre's physical activity coaches, Joe. She said I was past the need of a physio. I was more in the need of a PT. We started our hour-long session, every Tuesday, at the end of June. We worked on balance, core strength and flexibility. My flexibility was appalling, from lying in a hospital bed for so long, I couldn't even touch my toes, which I used to be able to do easily.

Lauren and I broke up in June. The last year had been hard on both of us and our relationship. I can't imagine how you deal with your boyfriend or girlfriend going through something like cancer treatment.

Bode rang our house phone at the end of June. He asked to speak to me to discuss my last scan. I was supposed to go to hospital to see him but due to coronavirus, this wasn't allowed. I put the phone on loudspeaker and set it on the kitchen table so mum and I could listen. He told me that the radiotherapy was having the desired effect. Whatever tumour was left in my brain, after surgery and chemotherapy, had shrunk. It had reduced in size. What great news, I couldn't have wished for anything better. He finished the phone-call and I burst into tears. Mum and I had a hug and we told dad the wonderful news.

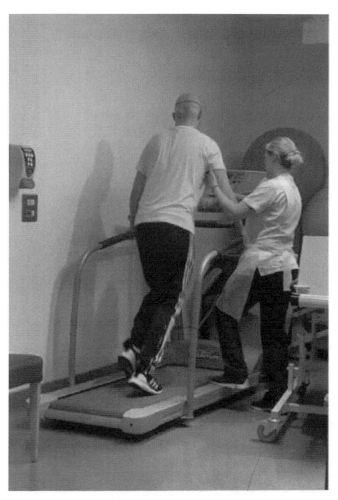

First time running in 6 months

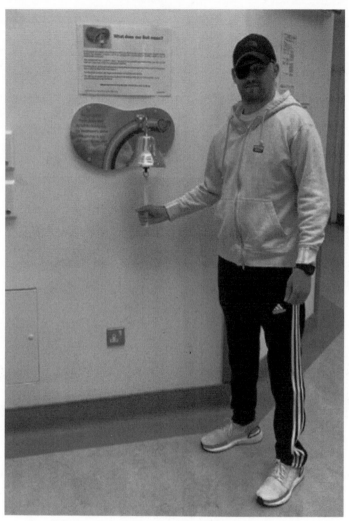

Ringing the bell after completing all cancer treatment

Out in my back garden with the decorations Ashlea had put up for me finishing treatment

My Birthday

The 11th of August came. My birthday. I turned 27 years of age. It was the first birthday where I have started to feel old.

When I came home from hospital in February Dad went and bought me the latest iPhone, as I didn't receive a Christmas present. This was to be my Christmas and birthday present combined, which I had no issues with whatsoever.

Even though I wasn't expecting any presents from my parents, they bought me shoes, so I had something to open from them on my birthday. I also got a 'Colin The Caterpillar' cake from Marks & Spencer. My favourite cake, one that I've had every year as long as I can remember.

My sister and her husband came to visit in the afternoon, along with my nanny and papa. They all brought gifts and hugs to say happy birthday and also to have some of my Colin cake.

My family and I hosted a 'Birthday BBQ' a few days after for some of my close friends. It was for my birthday celebrations but also a way of saying thank you to everyone who had been such great friends to me over the last year of my life. The worst year of my life.

Dad BBQed for everyone. I had bought beer for the guys and wine for the girls. We used a big ice bucket borrowed from Timmy - it was filled with ice, water and the drinks. Everyone could help themselves, whenever they wanted.

People brought presents and cards, all of which I have saved because it was an important birthday for me. My first after completing cancer treatment. The guys had all chipped in together to buy me something special: the new Arsenal home shirt. Arsenal are my favourite football team and have been since I was a little boy. My dad supported them and also my Granda.

Blowing out the candles on my Colin The Caterpillar birthday cake

My friends in our back garden for a birthday BBQ

My Arsenal shirt the guys bought me

INTERVIEWS

At the beginning of August I received a text message from Nigel Ringland. He asked me if I wanted to tell my story, on camera, for television, radio and the BBC website. Nigel was a reporter for BBC Newsline and BBC Sport. I have known him for a few years and have been interviewed by him many times for international and club hockey. Hockey isn't a very well documented sport within Northern Ireland, but Nigel has done a lot to improve the publicity of this. I said I would love to tell my story, if he felt it worthy enough for a spot on the evening news, or even the website.

A few weeks later, he came round to my house with a cameraman, and we set up in the back garden, to accommodate social distancing rules. We had a chat about the last year of my life., my cancer journey. He had emailed through questions that he would ask, so I could prepare answers, as I couldn't remember my time in Germany or the RVH and I needed my parent's assistance with this. We chatted for about 15 minutes and then did the same thing, but on camera.

The interview was to air later in the week. Firstly, on the radio and then on the news. Nigel warned me in advance that the TV interview might not be shown if the presenters went over their allotted time. My parents and I had the radio on during our dinner. The story was aired, and we listened. Then we turned on the TV to watch the news and my interview had made the cut. Albeit a shorter version of what was recorded, to meet the time constraints. The extended interview was released later that night on the BBC News for Northern Ireland website and the BBC Sport website. The online videos hit over 100,000 views combined. I received a flood of messages to my Instagram and Facebook pages. Men and women telling me they had cried at the video. This made me very emotional. Nigel had done an amazing job in helping me tell my story.

Later in August I received a message on Instagram from a page called 'The Helping Hand'. A girl called Vicki Walsh, from Dublin, asked would I be interested in doing an interview for her page, where she interviewed people who she deemed 'inspirational' and who made 'possibilities through a positive mindset'. She had seen my BBC interview with Nigel, and she had been asked by numerous people to get in contact with me. To let me tell my story. I agreed to Vicki's request. On the 7th of September Vicki drove from Dublin to my family home, in Waringstown, to interview me.

We went into the sunroom, to socially distance. Vicki set up her phone on a stand with a large circular light and directed it towards me on the sofa. She then sat down on the chair beside the sofa, and we started chatting. We discussed the last year of my life. The worst year of my life. We chatted for 30 minutes, she packed up and then left to go back to Dublin. She uploaded it online later that night to Instagram TV (IGTV) to be viewed by all her followers, I also reposted it to my IG story, for my followers to watch, if they wanted.

Soon after, Gareth Hanna, an old school friend, texted me to ask if I would do an interview for him on Friday 30th October as he was a reporter for The Belfast Telegraph. He was a friend of mine from Banbridge Academy, as we both played in the golf team together and he also played hockey. He was also in my sister's primary school class. Later in the week he came to the house, with a photographer, to take photos of myself and my family together. We did the photos first to allow the photographer to leave before we chatted. Ashlea and Timmy couldn't make this photo, so it was just my parents, myself, and our dog Lola, who took centre stage. Gareth interviewed me initially, in the sunroom. He then asked would my mum or dad speak to him. Mum offered to speak with him, and he asked for her thoughts on the last year. How we coped as a family. Mum mentioned how we have always been a mentally tough family which has helped through the cancer treatment and surgeries. I agreed with her. It really had helped, without a shadow of doubt. It was published at the start of November, a 2-page spread on the inside of the paper.

I then received a message into my Instagram inbox a week later, from a woman called Ali Wright-McCully. She was a reporter for a local paper, The Banbridge Chronicle. She asked would I be willing to do an interview for 'The Chronicle', as it was known, on my recovery, rehab and hopes for the future. I said I was happy to. If I did 100 interviews and it helped one person, it would be worthwhile. We did it over the phone and it made the back page of the paper, when it was printed. She ended the article by saying 'focus on the comeback, not the setback' and I thought, that is a great motto to start living my life by. A truer word couldn't be spoken. She was sending a photographer to the house later in the week, after we had our phone call. I knew him, Richard Hodgett. I had played golf with his son for one of the junior golf teams at Banbridge Golf Club. I also knew Richard from taking photos of local hockey matches in Banbridge. So, he set us up the way he wanted in the back garden with seats. Ashlea also made an appearance for this one.

With Lola and my parents for the Belfast Telegraph

With my family for the Banbridge Chronicle

STARTING WORK & SUNDAY TRAINING

Dad received a phone call from an old hockey manager of mine, Colly Walker, at the start of August. Colly, who was a maths teacher, had a job offer for me but he rang my dad to check if I was up to the task. Dad told him to ring me and ask, as it wasn't anything to do with him. My phone rang, "Hey Beller, I've an offer for you to think about." Colly said. "What do you think of working as a classroom assistant and hockey coach in the Academy?". Banbridge Academy was my old grammar school which helped to nurture and excel my hockey skills. I had won every schoolboy trophy possible and two 'All Ireland' titles, back-to-back, making us the best school 1st XI in the country. "I'd love to, Colly," I replied. It would give me a routine. My routine at this moment in time was to wake up at 10am, take my Keppra medication, which was time sensitive, it had to be taken at 10am and 10pm, 12 hours apart. I would go down and have breakfast, shower, then spend the rest of the day on the sofa, only moving to get a drink or food. Then I would go to bed at 9:30pm, take my Keppra up with me and take it at 10pm. I would sleep 11 and a half hours a night, straight through and have a nap on the sofa, for an hour in the afternoon. Not really a routine, as such. This job would give me structure, a sense of purpose, something to get out of bed for in the mornings. "Great, I'll let the school know and they will get back to you", he hung up.

The next day mum, dad and I were up in Portballintrae, at the north coast. We have an apartment up there and we had gone up for one night. We were sitting out at the picnic table in the glorious sunshine when my phone rang, "Hello, is that Matthew?" the voice said. "Yes, it is," I replied. "Matthew, this is Claire from the office in Banbridge Academy. I have spoken to Colin Walker and he has said you are interested in the job as a classroom assistant and hockey coach, is this correct?" she asked. "Yes Claire, I'd love to do it!" I replied. "That's brilliant, the job is yours. We will be in contact with a start date and other things as soon as possible." She hung up. I was ecstatic. Finally, something to do with my days, instead of lying on the sofa watching TV. I told mum and dad, who were sitting at the table with me, the great news. They were thrilled as well.

About a week later I received a letter in the post from Banbridge Academy. It said I would have an induction day on a Friday towards the end of August, for about an hour and I would then start full-time on the following Monday.

The Friday was very relaxed. We were only in the room for maybe a maximum of 90 minutes for a short PowerPoint presentation. I was to be the classroom assistant for a first-year class, year 8, and a third-year class, year 10, and also a hockey coach with whoever needed me or whatever team needed me.

We had borrowed a treadmill from our next-door neighbours, and it was in our garage. I was running twice a week, to a running programme written by my S&C coach, Lisa Costley. Since my balance still wasn't very good, I had to hold on to the handles on the side of the treadmill, to stop myself falling off.

The Monday came and I still didn't really know what I was doing. I was told to stick with my year 8 class for the first week, while they got settled into their new school and until I got my timetable.

At this stage my hair had been growing back for a while now and it was getting very long at the back. Mum's hairdresser was round at our house cutting mum and dad's hair at the start of September. After he had finished with them, I got him to tidy my hair up as it was a bit of a mess. There was no shape to it.

I woke up on Sunday the 13th of September. I went downstairs and had my breakfast as normal. I spoke to dad, "I want to go to Havelock, dad. I want to go to Havelock and run by myself, unaided."

It was a year, to the date, of my diagnosis. A year from hell. Anytime I had run in the hospital with my physio, Paula, it was on the treadmill, holding on to the sides, or I was running down the corridor, with her supporting me, a hand on my chest and a hand on my back.

Dad took me over to Havelock, the pitch at Banbridge Hockey Club. This was where I played all through my childhood and where I was the captain, the season before I moved to Germany.

I ran a couple of lengths of the pitch, wavering left and right, without knowing I was doing so. I only noticed it when I watched the video back that dad had recorded. I didn't know what I was doing, but I didn't care. I was back running unaided, another step on the road to normality.

When I got home, I went to the shower. I burst into tears. I was overjoyed, back being able to run unaided again. I cried for a good ten minutes, while the hot water hit my head and ran down my back. Crying is something I've learnt to do over the time period of my illness. Through the surgeries, cancer treatment and recovery. Before the last year, I hadn't cried since I didn't make the Olympic team, it was a rarity for me. The last year I can't remember how many times I've cried. I wouldn't be able to count them on both hands.

I had asked dad to video me running, so I could post it to my Facebook and Instagram pages. The response I received was incredible. The messages of support flooded into my Facebook and Instagram inboxes. Aoibhne, the wife of a close friend of mine and also previous teammate of Ireland and

Banbridge, Eugene Magee, messaged me. She's a qualified physiotherapist. She messaged to say she had noticed a few things wrong with my running. She offered to come down and reteach me how to run, since I was basically learning again from scratch. She wanted to come down and correct my technique, so I wouldn't be going back to hockey with any bad habits that might be detrimental to my game or might cause injury. This is what I meant earlier when I said the hockey community had been amazing in supporting me throughout my illness. What an offer, from a lovely family. I wasn't going to turn her down, not an offer like that.

That was the start of my Sunday training. I would go to Havelock every Sunday and do a bit of running, each week I would do a bit more than the previous. It also gave me time to play some hockey, the sport I love, with my parents. I know, it was nothing like playing a match, but it was a step closer to getting to that moment.

Aoibhne and I scheduled to meet at Havelock the following Sunday. We went down and I ran a couple of lengths with her shouting instructions at me. She stopped me and made me run like an aeroplane, with both arms out, like wings. I was running with my left arm a lot higher than the right, which obviously isn't normal. She then made me run with my hockey stick in my left hand, to take my left arm out of my running technique. This was alien to me since I always ran with it in my right hand, but her coaching technique worked. We decided to meet every 2-4 weeks, depending on Aoibhne's schedule but I would still go down every Sunday, with my parents, to run and to pass a ball around. Nothing would stop me getting back on that pitch. If it was sunny, I would run. If it was wet, I would run. I just wanted to play a hockey match again.

October came around and I was booked in for my first proper haircut with my old barber in Banbridge. I hadn't had a normal haircut in over a year and I was ecstatic about getting my hair back to normal. I got back into the car after my haircut and mum said to me "that's normal Matthew back again." Again, normality was resuming.

I had received a letter in the post a few weeks prior to the start of October. It was to let me know that it was time for my next scan. So, the Friday came, dad and I set off to the RVH. It was the same procedure as before, except this time I didn't have to have an x-ray before as they had my shunt settings from the last time. I just needed an x-ray after the scan.

I lay on the bed and waited for the dye to be injected into my bloodstream. The scan was finished after 30 minutes, and I was allowed to go home.

My second rehab session with Aoibhne at Havelock came around, on the 11th of October. She said to me "is there anything you want to work on today? Anything you need to relearn?". "I still can't get off the ground, back onto my feet, without someone giving me their arm, or a bit of furniture to hold on to" I replied. She had me go down on to the pitch in 'tabletop position'. On my hands and knees. She then explained how to get back on to my feet, since I seemed to have forgotten. "Bring your foot forward into a lunge position and from there step up to a standing position" she explained. I did it. It seemed so easy when she explained it simply. She made me do it a couple of times. Then she made me lie on my back and do the same thing again, except this time I had to roll over and get myself into that tabletop position. That was it, I could finally get back onto my feet by myself. Something which seems so simple but to me it wasn't.

A couple of weeks later, at the end of October, I went to Havelock again with my parents. I did my normal thing, my warmup, some simple running drills and played a bit of hockey with my parents. When I got home, dad called me over and gave me a hug. "I wasn't sure if I was ever going to see you run again," he said emotionally. It gave me a lump in my throat. "Well, you have dad, and you will watch me play a hockey match again too," I replied. We stopped our embrace, and I went up to the shower. I started crying. My own father wasn't sure if he would ever see me run again and I was an international hockey player. That was hard to hear. It brought all kinds of emotions out of me.

One day after I came home from work, I googled about brain haemorrhages, since I was a day away from having one apparently. It said 30-60% of people that have them then pass away. They don't recover from them. Dr Google isn't the best thing to check medical conditions with, but it was all I had. It makes me feel lucky to be alive. It makes me feel like I've been given a second chance, hence the name of this book.

First 'proper' Haircut with my barber Nathan

First session with Aoibhne at Havelock

Phone Calls

The house phone rang. It was Bode again, to chat about my last scan. He said there was no issue with the scan but there was scar tissue in my brain, and they couldn't see past the scar tissue, so there may be some residual tumour left behind the scar tissue after all the treatment. He explained there was 3 potential courses of action:

1. Keep scanning every 3 months. To check if there was any change to the tissue in my brain.
2. 'Cyber knife radiotherapy', which is a very high dose of radiation, directed to a very localised area and it would be a one-off treatment. This was to be sure, to be sure, to be sure. It would be targeted at the site of the scar tissue, in case there was anything residual, behind the scar tissue.
3. Surgery. Bode said this would be the last option. I also made it very clear I didn't want any more brain surgeries. I think 5 in 6 weeks is enough for my lifetime, and my family's.

Bode explained that my case had been sent off as a referral to Leeds, in England. This was the centre of excellence for this type of treatment, and we wouldn't hear anything for a few months as there was no immediate concern from the scan, so the treatment wasn't needed straightaway.

In a way I was slightly disappointed with this phone call. I knew of people who had been told 2 months after completing cancer treatment that they were in remission. The one word I had dreamt of hearing ever since I was told I had cancer. It seemed like a distant dream at this point, which made me sad, but I had to look at the positives. There were no concerns with the scan which was the main bit of news I was overlooking. I asked him about driving and he said I needed to contact the DVA to see what they said.

After the phone call with Bode I contacted the DVA and asked to be transferred to someone who could deal with my query regarding returning to driving. They said it had to be discussed with my oncologist, Bode. They would send me medical forms to fill in and then had to be sent back to them with my GP's signature, even though my GP had nothing to do with my treatment. My mum rang Bode's secretary and explained the situation. She said she would get in touch with Bode and they would write up a letter, which he would sign, stating in his eyes, I was fit to drive. I hadn't driven in over 14 months at this stage. I was relying on my parents, grandparents and sister to lift and lay me, to and from work and any other places I wanted or needed to go.

About a week later we received the medical forms from the DVA, we filled them in and dropped them into my GP's office, for him to sign. We received them back a few days later and posted them off ourselves to the DVA in England. I knew I wouldn't hear anything from them before Christmas or the New Year. I didn't care, the ball was rolling for me to get back driving, to get my independence back.

Near the end of November, mum's phone rang. It was Mr Weir, a consultant neurologist in the RVH, whose care I was under when I was admitted to hospital in Belfast. I don't remember my time in the RVH, so I didn't know what he looked or sounded like. We spoke for a few minutes, discussing my recovery and then he moved on to the reasons he called.

Keppra, my anti-seizure drug, was to be reduced by 250mg every 2 weeks. I was on 750 mg twice a day. After I received the prescription and tablets, I would start straight away. Start on 500mg tablets, twice a day. After 2 weeks I would then be reduced to 250mg for another 2 weeks. Then after another 2 weeks, it would stop. The last tablet to do with my cancer treatment, would be gone.

I asked him about driving and he said it shouldn't be an issue after seeing my BBC interview. He said I've had a miraculous recovery since I was so unwell when I was under his care. I didn't even speak to him when I was in the RVH, plus Bode was already on the case of me returning to drive.

The programmable shunts that are in my head are staying in. There is more chance of doing harm than good by taking them out; if they were taken out, I wouldn't be able to drive for another 6 months. Plus, they had no life span, so they could stay in.

The risk of surgery to remove whatever is left in my brain is too great. It would cause more damage than good to try and remove whatever is in there. He agreed with Bode and I, that surgery was a no go. I was really against it.

POSITIVE MENTAL ATTITUDE

I received a phone-call from Mark Cordner a P.E. teacher and the Master in Charge of boy's hockey at Banbridge Academy, at the end of November. Mark had been one of my coaches during my time at Banbridge Academy. He was the main reason 'The Academy', as it was known, was such a high profile and successful hockey school. He was a very driven and motivated individual, which rubbed off on all his players and students.

He was planning a 'chips, chaps and chats' afternoon during the senior boy's games on Wednesday the 25th. The idea of this was to talk about the importance of PMA, or a positive mental attitude. He asked me would I speak, for a few minutes about the important of having a PMA, something which helped me through my time in hospital and during my cancer treatment. He said I would be the ideal individual to talk about this and the students would be able to relate to it since they knew me personally. I immediately agreed.

The Wednesday came around. I had made a few bullet points of what I was going to say, I had looked over the notes numerous times during my break and lunch in work. I felt nervous, which was strange. Before I had gone into hospital, I was happy to speak in front of crowds. I didn't get nervous. I was used to doing interviews and speeches in front of crowds, for TV or radio.

I spoke for around 5 minutes about my time in hospital and previous experiences where having a PMA was important and helped me through difficult times. I finished speaking and received a large round of applause. I felt emotional. I looked over to the side and I saw my dad standing. Mark had invited him down to watch and told him not to let me know he was coming. I was very surprised to see him there, but very happy he could be there to see me speak to the players.

CHRISTMAS 2020

We had a normal family Christmas Eve. A Chinese with Ash, Timmy, my mum's parents, my parents and myself. We normally would go to my grandparent's house for it but this year my mum insisted we had it at our house. Food and drinks were flowing. We all had a lovely evening, and everyone went home for the night. They would all come back the next day, for Christmas Day.

I went to bed, ready to wake up in my own room and house for the first time in 2 years on Christmas Day. I burst into tears. Tears of joy. I was emotional and ecstatic to be waking up in my own bed, to have breakfast in my own house on Christmas morning. I cried for a good 10 minutes, before drying my eyes with my duvet, turning over and falling asleep.

I woke up at 8:30, which was early for me. I could hear noises downstairs, so I went down to see mum and dad already having breakfast. We all had a hug and wished each other a happy Christmas. I started to feel emotional, again, but I held it together. I couldn't have been happier to be in my own house for Christmas. Another step on the ladder to normality, which I loved. Each day was another step closer.

Ash and Timmy arrived a few hours later to exchange presents. They brought their dog, Bella, in her Christmas jumper, to play with Lola, they got on like a house on fire. We exchanged presents and hugs and waited for my mum's parents to arrive.

It was dinner time. Christmas dinner time. As I had done it 2 years before, it was my job to carve the turkey, under the guidance of my papa, Sydney. He had taught me 2 years previously which was the first time I had ever carved a turkey, but I had forgotten what to do. He talked me through the steps while watching over me and giving me a helping hand. I finished carving and everyone plated up. There was dessert after of course. My sister had made a cheesecake, like the year previously, except this year it was 'Terry's chocolate orange' flavour and there was also one of mum's Christmas puddings. Both went down a treat. When finished, I was stuffed. Talk about a food coma. Everyone moved to the sofas, to relax. We watched TV together. Nanny and Papa went home, and we got changed in to our 'comfies'. I came down from putting my pyjamas on and everyone was around the table for cheese and port. After the cheese and port, we moved back to the sofas.

Tiredness overcame me at 10pm, so I said goodnight to everyone before making my way to the kitchen to collect my Keppra tablet and glass of water, as I would take it in the morning before getting out of my bed. This was my last reduction in Keppra, I was down to two 250mg tablets a day for another 2 weeks then I would be finished all tablets to do with my cancer treatment. My dad followed me out to the kitchen. "You weren't the only one to cry last night in bed" he said. He told me how it meant so much to him to have me back home for a normal Christmas with the family. I know I was allowed out of hospital last year, to go to my sister's house but that wasn't 'normal', like this year. We had a hug, and I went up to my bedroom and got into bed after brushing my teeth. I started to cry again. I'd had the best day with my family. I didn't care about the presents, or the food, I was just happy to be back in my own house, surrounded by a loving family, for Christmas Day. I knew there would be some people in the world who wouldn't be as lucky.

The next morning came. Ashlea and Timmy had stayed the night. I waited for everyone to get up and I asked them if they wanted pancakes. Everyone said they would have a couple, so I whipped up my batter and made pancakes for everyone. I even made 2 mini pancakes for the dogs, one for Bella and one for Lola.

We just chilled out all day. We made ham and cheese toasties with the Christmas ham. No one was very hungry after the feast the day before and the pancake breakfast. After lunch, Ash and Timmy went home. For dinner we had round 2 of Christmas dinner and then that was Christmas over for another year.

Tuesday the 29th of December was my last running session of 2020. A year from hell. Dad took me to Havelock to run and play some hockey, like we had done for the last couple of months. The pitch was frozen, so I was unable to do any form of turning, shuttles or zigzag runs etc. I was still able to do straight line running and pass the ball with dad, but it wasn't the same. I needed to practise my turning, not my straight line running but I was just happy to be running again, and not sitting in a wheelchair, like I was last Christmas. This Christmas had been a lot happier in my eyes. Don't get me wrong, the previous Christmas, being able to leave hospital to be with my family was amazing, but nothing is as good as waking up in your own bed.

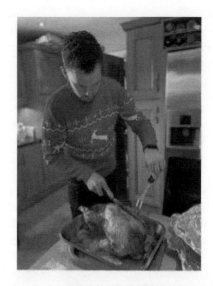

Me carving the turkey

The pancakes I made

Christmas 2019 vs Christmas 2020

The New Year

The 31st of December came around. I wasn't planning on staying up to midnight, I would be in my bed, catching my sleep, which my body needed.

Finally, 2020 was over. A year from hell. Surely 2021 couldn't be as bad?

I went to bed at 10:30pm. I went on to my Instagram to look at the messages I had received in reply to my story of the mojitos I had made for the family. One in particular struck a chord with me. My old house mate Luke, from my time in Belgium, had messaged me. I had posted saying how awful 2020 was and I couldn't wait for 2021 to start. He replied, saying for him, he saw it as the opposite of me. He said I came out of 2020 healthy, still a cheeky asshole and raring to go. He said I jumped a thousand barriers to get to where I am and said 2020 was my year of domination.

I hadn't looked at it like that. I just looked at it as an awful year. I watched my BBC sport interview, again. I teared up and started to cry. Tears, but tears of joy. One of the worst years of my life was over, finally.

The next morning after breakfast, I waited for the road in my housing development to thaw out. I put on my running clothes and running shoes. I wanted to start 2021 as I meant to go on. No longer looking back at what had happened. That was in the past, it was now time to focus on the future. 2021, my comeback year.

This was the longest I had run for unaided. I was severely out of breath. Any time I ran at Havelock, it was short runs, focusing on changing direction. It was also the first time I had ran on tarmac as every other time was either on the hockey pitch or on the treadmill. I finished my running and went back into the house. I sat on the sofa to catch my breath and have a drink. I then went to the shower, and I could feel my legs aching. I knew I would be sore in the morning, I could feel my calves seizing up.

The next morning when I got out of bed, I was sore. My hip flexors, glutes and calves felt like they were in pieces.

I ran again on Sunday afternoon. This time, I went back inside to have a drink. I wasn't out of breath as much as the Friday, which was a positive. I had been running once a week up until this point, maybe it was time to start doing more? When I lived in Germany, we would train 7 times a week, including gym sessions, plus 1, if not 2 matches at the weekend, but I was no longer a full-time athlete. I was still recovering from cancer treatment.

Friday the 8th of January came around. It was a big day in my eyes as it was the last time I was to take a Keppra tablet. I had been on it from my time in hospital in Germany. In Germany I would take 'absent seizures' or 'absences'. I would be having a conversation and would then just zone out for 10 or 15 seconds, just staring through you as if you weren't there, into the distance. Keppra couldn't just be stopped, it had to be reduced slowly in dosage. I hadn't had an absence since September 2019 in Germany. I was taking 1000mg twice daily there. When I was moved to the Royal Victoria Hospital in Belfast, Mr. Weir reduced it down to 750mg twice daily almost immediately and that's the dose I stayed on the whole way through my stint in hospital. The 8th of January was to be my last tablet at 9pm. It wasn't a tablet directly involved with my cancer treatment, but in my eyes it was. It was the last tablet to do with cancer treatment for me. It was a big step for me, on the road to normality.

The same day, I rang the DVA to check on the status of my medical forms which had been sent off to them earlier in

December, to get me back driving. I couldn't wait to start driving again, not having to rely on my parents to lift and lay me wherever I needed to go. To get my independence back. They had received the forms. Their medical team had ok'd everything, but the forms and case had been sent to an external occupational therapist company and they would contact me in due course. But with Covid-19, the postal service was very slow. I didn't know when I would hear about driving again.

On Monday the 11th of January I woke up around 9:15am and walked down the hallway to the bathroom. All I could hear was mum, from the kitchen downstairs saying, "Should I go up and wake him?". I looked at my phone and I had a photo sent from my sister with the caption 'Hi Uncle Matthew, I'm your new partner in crime'. I opened the message, and it was a photo of the cutest wee baby boy, that Ashlea had given birth to at 6:30 that morning, weighing 5lb 12 oz.

Ash had come round to our house during the summer, around dinner time, to tell us she was pregnant. Mum, dad and I were at the kitchen table, and she walked into the kitchen, handing mum and dad a wrapped present and a card. She handed me a card as well. I opened the envelope and the front of the card read 'you've been promoted'. I was very confused. I opened the card, and, on the inside, it read 'you've been promoted, from dog uncle, to human uncle' with a photo of a pregnancy scan. Mum and dad got a card with the photo of the scan too, and the present was a little baby grow with 'Baby Hall' written on the front of it. I stood up and hugged Ashlea. What amazing news. Apparently, I was upgraded, Ashlea saw me as her dog Bella's uncle.

Mum, Dad and I went to visit Ash, Timmy and the new arrival later in the week. We walked in and sat down, and Ash said "we have a name. He's going to be called Albie Timothy

John Hall." Mum cuddled him first, then passed him to me. I couldn't believe the size and fragility of him. Named Timothy, after his father, and John, after our father. Mum told me off, for cuddling him for so long, but I didn't want to let go. He was going to be my partner in crime.

We left and went home. We arrived home and dad's phone rang. It was his sister, Jenny. She was ringing to let dad know that their mum, my granny, had just passed away in her nursing home. She was 84 years of age and had dementia for the last 3 years. Dad said to me that he had lost his mum 3 years ago and he had been waiting for this day. So, in a way he was prepared for this, but who is ever prepared for losing their mother? He had visited her the week before and had said she was very frail, had lost a lot of weight and needed her hair cut. He said she barely opened her eyes, and her head was drooped the whole time he was visiting. He knew it wouldn't be long till her passing. In a way it was the best for her, she had no quality of life, moving from care home to care home. She was back with her husband.

The funeral was organised for Sunday the 17th of January. Due to the coronavirus pandemic, the funeral was held graveside. An outdoor service, with only 15 people allowed. The minister, from her church spoke very highly of her. My mum was teary, so I had my arm around her for most of the service. Her crying made me shed a tear or two also. It was a lovely, quiet service, with no fuss. Ideal for my granny. She never liked anything extravagant.

The 28th of January was my sister's 30th birthday. It was the start of a year of big milestone birthdays. Ashlea was turning 30. My papa was turning 90 in July and my dad was turning 60 in October, plus the birth of little Albie, what a year 2021 was going to be. Mum had ordered a special cake for Ashlea from a bakery in Banbridge. On the Thursday we went round to Ashlea and Timmy's house with the cake and

Timmy had a bottle of champagne for us to enjoy. Mum's parents came also. We gave Ashlea her presents and had a meal. This had been preordered from a restaurant in Belfast and delivered that morning. This was the new 'eating out' during Covid. We then had cake and bubbles, and left to go home.

I went back to Havelock on the following Sunday with my parents to run and play hockey. Over the previous few weeks, I had been having negative thoughts whether I would ever get back to the level I was at. I wasn't sure if I'd ever play international hockey again, which is all I wanted to do. Not even international, but just any level. Would I make it back on to the pitch for a match?

I went to Havelock and did some more running, changing direction and hockey with my parents. It put my mind at ease, after finishing I felt positive. I knew I would play hockey again and I would try my best to play international hockey again.

Recent Scan

The 1st of February was my next scan. I had received a letter the week prior, letting me know it was coming up in the RVH.

The same week I received my letter I was doing my at-home body weight exercises. I had gotten off the floor and sat in my desk chair. I felt a build-up of pressure in the back of my head, and I got dizzy, which really worried me. I told my parents about it, but my mum reassured me that it was nothing. I knew my scan was coming up, so I stopped thinking about it. I knew I would find out what was going on in my head soon enough.

The scan came around and it was the same routine as my last scan. A coronavirus questionnaire before the scan, to make sure I had no symptoms or been in recent close contact with a person who had tested positive. A cannula was inserted into my arm, for the contrast dye to be inserted through during the scan. The scan would then take place and then I would have an x-ray after the scan to check the settings on my shunts hadn't changed. Everything went well, no changes were found in my shunts, so I was allowed to leave and go home.

One week after the scan, our house phone rang. Mum rushed into the room and handed me it, saying she thought it was Bode. "Hello is that Matthew? It's Bode here to talk about your last scan." I wasn't expecting this call because I normally would have received a letter in the post stating I had a phone consultation coming up with the date and time. My last scan also took 3 weeks for the results to come through. Bode started to explain the results of the scan.

The query over the scar tissue that had shown up in my previous scan which meant I might have had to go to Leeds for the cyber knife radiotherapy had been assessed again by Leeds, for the second time. They had looked at my previous scan and this scan and had decided that it was just a blood vessel surrounded by scar tissue and they were happy that no tumour remained so I wouldn't have to go to Leeds for the radiotherapy treatment. I would be scanned every 3 months until the following April, two years after finishing cancer treatment, then it would change to every 6 months. He asked me did I have any questions. "What about remission Bode?" I asked. "Is there any possibility of being told in the near future that I am in remission?". "The type of cancer you have Matthew, has the best chance of coming back within 2 years, so I won't be able to tell you that you are in remission until that point, which will be at the end of this year, at the earliest" he replied. We finished our conversation and he hung up the phone. What great news. No tumour remained. The best possible news at that point. I saw dad was already in tears. I got up and hugged him and then mum joined the embrace. The news still hadn't sunk in with me. About half an hour later the postman put the post in through our letterbox and funnily enough the letter about my phone call to discuss the results was in it.

A Return To Driving?

The hockey season, both nationally with the EYHL and domestically with the provincial leagues were cancelled in line with the ongoing coronavirus pandemic. This meant I wouldn't be able to play any matches this year, if I got myself into any reasonable physical shape to do so. All I wanted to do was get back on the hockey pitch, to play a match, in the sport I loved and knew so well. This made me upset but there was still a chance of a cup competition being played provincially after Easter with a chance of the season being extended into June or July. When I went home, I went to the shower and cried. Tears of joy - I was ecstatic being back on the pitch again.

For some reason I had been very gassy for a few weeks. In the mornings especially I would belch a lot at breakfast time. On three occasions within a week, I had been eating my breakfast and the trapped wind I had in my stomach, caused me to bring back up what I had been eating. I also hadn't been eating as much. Mum phoned Bode's secretary and she checked with him what to do. He said to start back on the Lansoprazole tablets I had been on when taking steroid tablets. It's a medication used to reduce stomach acid. I had a few left over from my previous treatment so I started them the next morning.

I had received a letter in the post from my GP surgery in Lurgan. I was to receive my first coronavirus vaccine as I was deemed in the 'at risk' category. I was surprised in a way. The previous summer when the radiotherapy was still working in my system, I would have thought I was more at risk but now not so much, but I wasn't going to say no. On the 18th of February I went to The Baptist Church in Lurgan to receive my first vaccine. I went to the entrance hall, gave my name and date of birth and was taken straight into one of the booths. I received my vaccine and my vaccine card which had the name of the vaccine I received and the date of my next vaccine which was 10 weeks after the first vaccine.

I went home and there was a letter lying on the floor when I walked through the door addressed to me from the DVA. I knew it was to do with my return to driving as I had previously phoned them 3 times trying to get an answer. I opened the letter and started reading. They said I shouldn't start back driving as I didn't meet the criteria and I should reapply in September of this year. What a disappointment. All I wanted to do was get back driving to get my independence back and not need my parents to transport me anywhere I wanted to go. It said on the letter I should consult with my GP for the reasoning behind the decision as a letter had been sent to him. I rang the GP, and he couldn't take anymore calls that day so I would have to ring back the next morning.

I rang back the next day and was put on a list for the doctor to ring me back. He rang me back an hour later. I explained the situation to him, and he went to check their post, but they hadn't received any letters. He said to ring back the following week. I also told him about my belching problem and that I was starting back on my lansoprazole tablets as per Bode's guidance. He said to stick with the tablets for a couple of weeks and see what the outcome was.

Dad did some research and found something on the DVA website that stated you couldn't drive for 2 years after initial treatment, which would have been my surgery in Germany, in September 2019, so the two-year waiting made sense. I would have to reapply in September 2021. I wouldn't know until the doctor received that letter explaining the reason. Why couldn't they just tell me? Maybe it was to do with my Keppra tablets? I don't think in my application to get my licence back that I, or my oncologist's letter had stated that the medication had started to be reduced. If it was the Keppra tablets, I would definitely be appealing, as I had finished them over a month ago. If it was the two-year rule, then there was nothing I could do but wait.

A week later I got in contact with my GP again and he confirmed the reason for my licence refusal. It was 2 years post initial treatment. September 2019 was my initial surgery so I would have to reapply in September 2021 for my licence. I guess my parents had a few more months of driving me around.

First Session Back

Tuesday 20th April was a big day for me on my road to recovery and normality. It was my first training session back on the pitch in a group dynamic. I hadn't been on a pitch with a team for 587 days. That's a long time. I was joining in with the Banbridge Hockey Club Men's 1st XI training session. I had been in contact with the coach, Scott, who used to be the assistant coach for the men's 1st team when I played for Banbridge before I moved abroad, to ask if it was okay for me to come down as only certain numbers were allowed on the pitch due to coronavirus restrictions. Thankfully there was a space for me. I did my own physical warmup, some shuttles to work on my change of direction and some stick and ball before the team started their drills. The drills were far too advanced for me at this stage but Scott let me take part by adjusting one of the routines so I could stand on a tyre to receive and pass the ball, to keep the drill flowing. I only stayed for an hour, if even, but the joy it gave me to be back on a pitch, with a team, in a team environment, was immeasurable. Being told by other players you made a good pass, something so small and something you wouldn't think about, I didn't realise how much I had missed it. I couldn't wait for the day that I would play a match. When I went home, I went to the shower and cried. Tears of joy - I was ecstatic being back on the pitch again.

The next week, I went back to training again. James Corry, another hockey player who had gone through cancer treatment for testicular and lung cancer told me that he didn't train, he just played a match for the 2nd XI and he faceplanted three times during the match. My second training session I tried to do a bit more. We did a shooting drill which needed the ball to be passed and received on the move before the shot. I entered the D to take my shot. The ball got caught up around my feet and I tried to hit it on my reverse anyway. I got tangled up and faceplanted. Normally if that had have happened before I fell ill, the guys would have laughed at me and shouted some abuse but since everything that had happened they all were worried and were asking was I okay. They came over to ask if I needed a hand off the ground but at least now, I knew how to get back on to my feet, thanks to Aoibhne. I had to text James after I got home, to say I didn't faceplant in my first session back, but I did the second.

A few weeks prior, Aoibhne had told me to ask my GP for a referral to the neuro physio team in Lurgan hospital. She rang them to check on my referral and they said I was at the bottom of a very long list, as I was able to do a lot more than others. Other people were learning how to get out of bed, and I was trying to get my balance back to somewhat normal. They gave her some exercises to go through with me, so we met at Havelock a couple of weeks later to go through them. To say they were basic, would be an understatement. My body had completely reset in everything. My core barely existed and that's why these exercises were so basic. It wasn't doing a plank, the core of all core exercises, no pun intended. It was to work on my inner, deep core, which needed strengthening, before anything else should be done. She explained the exercises and told me I was to do them every day and we would re-convene a few weeks later.

I asked was I still able to go to training, since my core was so weak. She agreed, as long as I knew my limitations and where my body was at that moment in time. Not to try and push too hard, too soon. I told her I did know where my limitations were and I was just trying to do something more each week, no matter how small, just to take a step in the right direction, back to normality.

We spoke about how people said to me "It's good to be alive, isn't it?". Of course it was. I knew I had been given a second chance but all I wanted to do was be back to my best and playing for Ireland with the dream of playing in the Olympics. She said if I ever needed to vent, with profanity, to go to her husband Eugene at a training session because she knew how frustrating it was for me, to be as immobile as I was. Also, my parents wouldn't be a fan of me venting and using swear words.

A week later I was taking part in another session with BHC. I took part in a 5v5 half pitch game. This was my first-time taking part in any kind of 'contact training' as it's known. It made me realise how far I had to go to get back to any kind of normal hockey, by my standards. I had no peripheral vision. I had to focus very hard on stopping the ball, and then figure out what I would do with it. Before I fell ill, I knew what I would do with the ball before it came to me. I knew I would stop it and where it would be for me to pass it to someone, or run with it, if needed. That had completely vanished. In one way, I was very happy to be back playing in matches, but in another, I couldn't believe how bad I was. I came home and went to the shower and burst into tears. This time it was anger, not happiness.

Josh and I before training

The same week, I was going to take part in my first gym session. Not bodyweight exercises, like I had been doing, but using weights. My next-door neighbour, Craig, had transformed his garage into a gym and had said I could use it as much as I wanted, to help with my recovery. My S&C coach had given me a basic program to follow, twice a week. I did 2 sessions that week, 3 days apart. I woke up the morning after my first session and my body was aching. Talk about DOMs (Delayed Onset Muscle soreness). I knew I would be sore, 20 months without lifting a weight, something which I used to love. But I didn't expect to be this sore. But again, another step on the road to normality.

ANOTHER SCAN

Mum had received a phone call on a Monday, to say my next scan was that Wednesday. Weird, since I was always told about my scans via letter. Was something wrong? Had something come up they wanted to check?

I went down for the scan. Same routine as before, scan and then an x-ray after to check the levels on my shunts. This is the first time the settings had changed, which meant I had to get them changed back. They had to contact the neuro team in the RVH. A neurosurgeon came down and said to me "hello Matthew, it's been a while." I had no idea who he was, but he must have checked me when I was in the RVH for my tests. He couldn't get the device, to change my shunt settings, out of the case. The case had broken. He went away and came back half an hour later, having to break open the case to get the machine out. He did what he needed to do, and I was allowed to leave. Over 3 hours after I had arrived, my longest scan yet.

The next week I met a good friend Philip Doyle for coffee. He was the year above me in school and played hockey, but I knew him as I played for the same team. I, along with a couple of the better players from my year, played for the year above. He was a doctor for the NHS, but he was currently a full-time rower, training for the Tokyo Olympics. I hadn't seen him from the previous summer when he came to visit me at home. He said to me he couldn't believe the change in me, that I was 5 times further on than he had expected. He had also seen me in hospital the week after my chemotherapy had finished. Apparently, I had told him how I wanted to be back playing hockey, back in the Irish team within a few months of leaving hospital and finishing my radiotherapy and all cancer treatment. He said that back then, he just nodded his head and agreed, but in the back of his head he was thinking 'yeah right'. He didn't have the heart to say that I was being too ambitious then, but he told me it now.

I'd received another letter as I needed to get a blood sample done at GPs for tumour markers. This would be sent off to a lab and I would get the results at a later date. It was a way of double checking all the tumour was gone, as I'd been told in my last scan it was.

The week after my bloods were done, I was supposed to receive a phone call, from Bode, with results of my MRI scan. For some reason it was cancelled – probably because of covid but he sent a letter stating the scan of my head and spine remained clear, with no sign of active disease at all and everything remained reassuring. What great news to hear. The news was an early birthday present for my mum as it was her birthday the next day.

Shane O'Donoghue, a teammate from the Irish Men's squad came to visit me one morning before their training session. I hadn't seen Shane since I fell ill, but he had been in constant contact with my dad throughout my entire time in Germany and throughout my hospital stay and treatments in Belfast. He was the main reason for me moving to KHC Dragons in Belgium, he played for them when I had signed my pre-contract. He came to visit, and he brought my shirts that I would have worn had I stayed in Belgium. They were signed by the team as a get well present from the club.

I asked Shane would I have gotten the healthcare like I did in Germany, with the MRI scan and next day emergency surgery. He said I wouldn't have gotten the care in Belgium because the health system was nowhere near as efficient as Germany. That's scary to think about. If I had had a brain haemorrhage it would have been the toss of a coin whether I had lived. As my dad has always said, I was in the right place at the right time.

Bode rang a couple of weeks later, as he said he would. He rang to let me know about my blood test results and to see if I had any questions to ask him. He told me the blood test had come back clear, with no sign of tumour, or active disease. Everything was going in the right direction, towards remission, the one word I'd wanted to hear, since being told I had cancer. He also said my next scan would be in August and he would get me a CT scan to see if they could pinpoint the reason for my belching and random throwing up in the mornings. Would this MRI scan show that I would be in remission? Here's hoping…

Me with my playing shirts

Shane and I

PRESEASON

Preseason came around for Banbridge hockey club. They would train Tuesday and Thursday nights and a Saturday morning. I only trained the weeknights because I was going to the gym every Saturday morning and I wanted to keep that up.

One of the first sessions, we did a simple 3-man weave from the halfway line to the circle, ending with a shot. A very simple pass and move drill I had done hundreds of times with different teams. One I could normally do in my sleep. I did a few reps of the drill before John Clarke, one of the coaches, who was an ex senior international player and coach, pulled me to the side. He told me to stop focusing on finishing the drill and focus on doing the first pass and a second pass and then he said I should stop. He said my head wanted me to do one thing, since I knew the drill like the back of my hand, but my body couldn't cope with what my head wanted to do. He was completely right. My body and movement just weren't what they used to be when I was playing at the top level. He was right, but it annoyed me. Not being able to do such a simple drill was very frustrating. I got home and had a shower and went to bed. Josh texted me asking what was up, as he could sense I was annoyed leaving training. I explained to him the reason for my frustration, and he told me to go easy on myself. He said that people who have been in my position, some have never walked again, let alone run, or gone to the gym, and there I was trying to get back to playing at the top level of the sport, not even two years after my diagnosis. Again, he was right. I burst into tears and cried myself to sleep.

A letter arrived about my next scans. I had my CT scan one week and my MRI the next. I also had to get my bloods done again at my GPs.

I had a CT scan of my abdomen, to find out what was causing my random throwing up. It was very quick, and I was home before I knew it, as it was done in Craigavon Area Hospital. I would get the results along with my MRI results.

The next scan came around and the same thing happened with my shunts as the last time. They had changed settings, which meant I had to wait to have them changed back. It didn't work on the first attempt, so the technician brought me up to my old ward in the RVH. We had to check it all was done correctly on the computer just to make sure it was right. People had told me about my ward in the RVH, that it was a bit depressing, and they weren't wrong. It was very dark and dreary. It was - probably for the best that I don't remember it compared to The City Hospital. The shunts got changed back and I was allowed to leave, until my next appointment, which was for my eyes.

A few weeks later I returned to see about my eyes. I hadn't seen her in a year. She told me at my last appointment that I had 18 months of healing and then the healing would level off. My eyesight had changed from being double vision, to about 1.2x. But I thankfully knew what the real image was as the extra shadow was just like a hologram.

The ophthalmologist had said there was no change in my eyes from my previous appointment. She also said they could put me on a waiting list for a minor surgery on the 4th nerve of my bad eye, to bring the shadow back in. I wasn't sure if I wanted another surgery, even if it was a minor one.

MEETING BODE, AGAIN

The hospital had started to take face to face consultations again. I hadn't seen Bode, my oncologist, in 18 months. My parents and I went to the waiting room after signing in for my appointment. We sat for half an hour before being called to a separate room. On the walk to the room, we bumped into a member of staff who had worked with me during my time in The Cancer Centre. She couldn't believe how I looked, she barely recognised me.

I went in to see Bode and he said the same. Apart from walking in with my parents, he wouldn't have recognised me. He was used to seeing me, in a wheelchair, with no hair and a big fat round face from the steroid medication. He couldn't believe how well I looked.

He said there were no issues with the MRI scan and everything was moving in the direction that he would have hoped for.

He said the CT scan in Craigavon also showed nothing out of the ordinary, but they could investigate further by performing an endoscopy if I wanted, to just double check. I was put on the waiting list for the procedure but Bode said it would be a while, since I wasn't an emergency.

He asked how things had been going since I last saw him. I told him I was back training and, in the gym, twice a week. He asked how hockey was going and I told him how frustrating it was being back. My head wanting to do one thing but my body not being able to cope. He said I would get there, where I wanted to be. He said he knew how determined I was and after making it as far as I already had, I would only keep going in the same direction. I wasn't sure but it was nice to hear.

A couple of weeks later I received a call from Lurgan Hospital. They'd finally gotten back to me about my referral for neuro physio. I made an appointment for the following week.

Dad brought me to the hospital and the physio, Siobhan, rang my phone when it was time to go in. She brought me to their physio room, which was scarily similar to Paula's in The City Hospital. Siobhan did a few tests with me to see if what I had described to her on the phone was true. I had told her my balance was greatly affected, so she tested the exercises that Aoibhne had given me and then gave me more to do. She told me to go home and continue doing the exercises every day and I made an appointment to go back to her in a month time. This would continue over the coming months.

At a previous training session, one of the coaches said I would find a certain drill very difficult, because of my footwork and how poor it was. After 5 minutes he came over to me and said he couldn't believe the difference in my footwork and changing of direction. I told him it was down to the balance exercises I had been doing. I said it would hopefully keep improving with more balance work, which brought a big smile to his face.

I'd also received a letter about the endoscopy, the procedure Bode had put me on the list for. They'd had a cancellation so could take me at an earlier date. I had to take a Covid test a few days before the procedure. My first Covid test, what a horrible thing it is. Who likes a swab being shoved to the back of your throat and up your nose?

I went to Belfast City Hospital later in the week to have the procedure done. I was offered sedation but decided against it, as I'd have to stay in hospital for an hour extra before being allowed to go home. After the procedure started, I regretted my decision. I had to bite on a mouthpiece with a hole in it, which was to allow the camera to be fed into my mouth and my throat. To me, the camera looked huge. My throat was sprayed with some kind of numbing agent, which made no difference whatsoever. The camera was fed down and I immediately started coughing and retching. The nurse stopped and asked me to stop coughing as she couldn't do the procedure if I was coughing, but I couldn't help it. The procedure only lasted for 5 minutes, possibly the longest 5 minutes of my life. There was one nurse looking at the computer screen which had the camera feed on it, one was feeding the camera down my throat, one was holding one of my hands and one was giving me a back rub to try and make me relax, which didn't help me at all.

Finally, the camera was taken out and I could stop retching. They found a hiatus hernia just above my stomach. The reason behind my morning belching and random throwing up. They told me to ring my GP and get the medication I was on, changed over to a different type to see if it helped. It would be a trial-and-error basis, but at least something was found.

I went back out to the car and mum asked me how it was. "Awful" I said. She laughed. She had the same procedure done a couple of years before as she also had a hiatus hernia. She didn't want to tell me how bad it was and couldn't believe I didn't have sedation.

DRIVING

I received a letter from the DVA. I ripped it open, and the first paragraph stated I had been granted a licence for a year. A year? Why only a year? To be honest, it didn't matter. I was allowed to drive again.

I picked up the phone and rang the DVA. I wanted to check if I could drive straight away or if I needed to wait for my physical licence to arrive. They said I had to wait; in case I was stopped by the police. Apparently, it could take 3 more weeks for it to arrive. I'd been told I could drive, but I couldn't. How frustrating.

Thankfully my licence arrived the following week. Again, I rang the DVA, asking why it was only a year. They said it was granted on medical grounds and I would have to reapply in a year to then be given a licence for 3 or maybe 5 years. I didn't care, this was another step on the road back to normality.

Mum rang her insurance company to get me on her insurance. It wasn't until the following day that I was finally allowed to drive her car, while I waited to purchase my own.

I waited until I had finished work and I drove dad and myself into my grandparents in Lurgan, a short 5-minute drive away. Dad kept telling me to move right as I kept veering to the left.

That night, I drove myself to hockey training. I didn't get above 50mph, I was nervous. On the way home I was driving around a corner to the left, and I hit the grass and quickly made it back on to the road. Maybe dad was right about the veering to the left…

Just like everything else in my recovery, this was going to

take time. That dreaded 'T' word, which I desperately hated. Time to go back to normal. More waiting. But at least normality was a step closer. No more relying on my parents for transport when I needed to go somewhere, or relying on friends to pick me up and drop me off.

Later in the week I drove to watch my new girlfriend Jane play hockey just outside of Belfast. This meant driving on the motorway for the first time in over two years. I'll never forget driving on that road for the first time, trying to navigate between 4 lanes with cars passing me on either side.

Dad, mum, and I went to pick up my own car the following week. Finally, I had my independence back. Apparently, dad asked mum on their drive home without me if she thought they would ever see the day I would drive again.

I spoke to mum and dad in the kitchen one night and I said how I wasn't up to much in the RVH. Mum laughed when I said I wasn't up to much (even though I don't remember, just from hearing things people have said from having visited me). I asked why she laughed, and she said "You said you weren't up to much. You weren't up to anything." She said her and dad had thought they would have to convert one of the living rooms in our house into my downstairs bedroom and care for me fulltime. How scary is that?

Me and my first car post treatment

REMISSION

I'd had another scan, same procedures as before and thankfully this time the shunts hadn't changed.

The house phone rang about a week later, it was a woman's voice. Dr Carser, Bode's right hand woman as Bode was off. She said they couldn't be more delighted with me and how everything was going. There had been no sign of active disease for months.

I asked her, did that mean I was in remission? She said they didn't use that term anymore, but if I wanted to use it I could, they used the term 'cured'. I was definitely going to use it. It's the one word I had wanted to hear since I was told I had cancer.

I was to have another scan in 3 months and after that, they would go to 6 monthly scans. The best news to hear a few days before Christmas. An early Christmas present for my family and I. I rang Jane to tell her the wonderful news.

NORMALITY

My dad had received a text message from Doug Anderson, one of the captains of the teams in Banbridge Hockey Club. He asked if I wanted a runout by the end of the season. Of course, I said yes, it had been nearly 2.5 years since I had last played a match.

I was supposed to play for the 4th XI team one Saturday at Havelock Park, the home of Banbridge Hockey Club, my home club, the club where I had captained the 1st XI before I moved to play in Germany. Unfortunately, the opposition pulled out last minute and the wait went on. Was I not meant to be back on the pitch, playing a match?

A couple of weeks later, the 5th XI were playing at home. They were playing before the 1st XI played Lisnagarvey, one of the biggest rivalries in Irish hockey. A game I had always loved playing in when I was fit and healthy and playing for the 1st XI. I was asked if I wanted to play for the 5s, of course I said yes, it was their last match of the season.

The Saturday came and I woke up nervous. Me? Nervous for a hockey match? When I was playing professionally and internationally, I didn't get nervous. Playing in the World Cup in India in front of 12000 people I wasn't nervous but for my first match back, my first match in 2.5 years, I was nervous. I had texted Nigel Ringland who had done my BBC interview 18 months previously, as he said he wanted to be there for my first game back. He came down with a camera man and videoed my comeback game.

The match was enjoyable, emotional and frustrating all in one. I had to take myself off in the third quarter for a rest because I was so unfit. We won 2-0, thankfully.

The final whistle was blown and a few of my teammates came to hug me and congratulate me for getting back on the pitch for a match. The 1st XI walked on for their match, and everyone came over and congratulated me with hugs and high 5's.

I started to walk off the pitch and a few tears had started to roll down my cheeks, I could see my family and friends who had come to watch making their way over to me, so I pulled it together.

Nigel called me over for an interview. He asked me how it was and how it felt to be back on the pitch. I struggled to hold back tears. He asked what I found difficult now after my illness and I explained my mobility on the pitch and my eyesight were causing me issues. I said I needed to be more realistic with my goals now. Before I started back to hockey after falling ill, I had dreams and aspirations to be back in the Irish team and go back to Germany to play a thank you season for CHTC. I now realised those goals were probably out of reach, but I would never stop dreaming about them. They would always be the end goal, attainable or not.

Even when I was in hospital, lying in bed not really moving, all I wanted to do was play a match. There had been a lot of times, a lot of dark days where I didn't think that day would ever come, but it had.

2.5 years previously my family were told I might not ever walk or talk again, and there I was, having just played a hockey match.

People have told me over the course of my recovery how inspirational it is, to see me doing things that people said I might never do again.

I don't see it as inspirational. I just see it as someone getting over an illness and getting back to the sport they love. Nothing inspirational about it.

But that was it, normality had finally resumed.

Albie and I after my match

My family and I after my first match

Me after my first match with the new addition of my scrum cap

Jane and I

Me with my grandparents

Full Circle

About a month and a half after my first match, my parents and I finally got back to Germany, to see and thank everyone for being so kind to us when I was in hospital there.

We flew on a Thursday afternoon, arrived in Düsseldorf, collected our hire car, and drove to the city of Krefeld, where CHTC, my old club, was situated.

On the drive, while I was navigating to the club, I started tearing up in the back seat. The memory of the drive from Düsseldorf to the club, one I would have made hundreds of times. I don't know why, but it just made me very emotional.

We drove to the club, the guys had finished their training session and were inside having a team meeting. The coach and manager knew we were coming, but the players didn't.

I was waiting outside the meeting room for them to finish their meeting when one of the players opened the door to let some air into the room. He saw me and the look of shock on his face, at me standing there, was incredible.

Guess that was the surprise ruined?

Thankfully the team had finished their meeting before the weekend's matches. I walked into everyone clapping and standing to hug me, some guys in tears, some guys I didn't even know in tears. Ronan, the coach, introduced me and said a few words about who I was, what had happened a couple of years ago and that I was there to watch them be promoted back into the 'Erste Bundesliga' (first division), having been relegated the previous season.

A crate of beer was opened, we all had a drink and a toast, we chatted to everyone and then moved outside for a photo.

While outside, my old assistant coach, Basti, was at the end of one of the pitches, coaching the ladies team. He saw me and his jaw hit the pitch. He walked off the pitch and gave me a hug. 'Matty, I can't believe it's you. I didn't think I'd ever see you again' he said. He started to cry which made me cry. How sad is that? He didn't think he'd ever see me again.

Everyone caught up, but my parents and I had to leave to go check-in to our apartment. We said our goodbyes and said we would see them on Saturday for their first match of the weekend.

The next day we had an appointment to see Prof. Scholz again. He was the person who had performed my surgeries. We drove to the hospital and waited for him to see us. He said it was great motivation to see me again because he rarely saw patients after their surgeries as they would move hospital or go home. I thanked him for everything. The man had saved my life, what do you say to someone who has done that?

That evening we took my old manager, Perdita, and her son, Linus, out for dinner as a thank you for being so kind to my parents when they were over during my time in hospital. She had sorted them with a car and accommodation and the only thing they had to pay for was food and petrol. It just shows the kindness the club had shown to my family and I during my time there. It was my second home. We went back to Perdita's house after dinner for a drink and she handed me a bag. A bag with my new playing shirts I would have worn if still playing there. She told me I had to wear them over the weekend to support the guys.

The next day we went to watch the men play their first match of the weekend. If they won both matches, they would be promoted back to the top division. Thankfully they won -

one more on the Sunday and they would be back where they belonged.

We went out for dinner on Saturday night too, with Philip and Nicky - the people who gave mum and dad their flat to stay in while I was in hospital. We talked about everything that had happened and we said thank you for looking after my parents for 5 weeks.

The next day we went to watch the second match of the weekend. Again, they won, meaning they were promoted. We all celebrated on the pitch, and I was included in the team huddle and team photos after the game. They still saw me as part of the team. I started to tear up again.

After the match, everyone went back to the club to celebrate. Beers were flowing, the sun was out, and my family and I were back in my second home. Sadly, we had to head back to the airport to drop the car back and catch our flight home. I went around and said bye to everyone. Hugs and high fives and again, more tears. I told them it wouldn't be another 2.5 years before coming back again, and I meant it.

We left and got our flight back home. That was it. Dad said that was it: 'full circle'. Meaning we had completed the circle of me falling ill, being treated, getting better, and coming back to where it all had started. To my second home - the place that saved my life.

To the place that gave me my second chance.

The team and I

The team and I after promotion

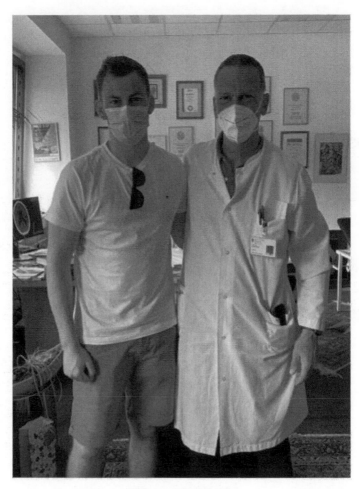

Professor Scholz and I

Me in my playing shirt

Second Chances

ABOUT THE AUTHOR

Matthew Bell was a professional field hockey player for Crefelder HTC in Krefeld, Germany when he and his family's lives were turned upside down when he was diagnosed with a germinoma – a slow growing brain tumour which had been there from before birth. This book documents his recovery and his challenging path back to competing in the sport he loves and played for a living.